Carnivore Diet Cookbook for Easy Recipes

2000 Days of Simple and Delicious Meat-Based Meals with a 30-day Meal Plan

Blake Lucas

Library of Congress Cataloging-in-Publication Data Names: Blake Lucas, author.

Title: Carnivore Diet Cookbook for Easy Recipes: 2000 Days of Simple and Delicious Meat-Based Meals with a 30-day Meal Plan

Description: First Edition. | Includes index.

Subjects: Carnivore diet Cookbook, Healing, Cooking (Natural foods).

Cover design by [Hollybookstore]

Interior design by [Blake Lucas]

Photography by [Blake Lucas] [Shark Publications]

Printed in [USA] First Printing, [08,2024]

This book is dedicated to everyone on their journey to health and wellness through the Carnivore diet lifestyle. May you find joy, inspiration, and deliciousness on every page. While the author and publisher have made every effort to ensure the accuracy and completeness of the information conveyed in this book, they assume no responsibility for errors, inaccuracies, omissions, or any inconsistency herein.

Any slights of people, places, or organizations are unintentional. The recipes and content in this book are intended as a helpful guide and should not replace medical, nutritional, or health advice from a professional. Readers should consult a healthcare provider before starting any new diet or exercise program.

CONTENTS

MEATS (BEEF, PORK, LAMB, ETC)

Free ebook of Tips for Staying on Track with the Carnivore Diet

This ebook will guide you through all the points given below in detail. So, sign up and get your free ebook right now.

Meal Prep Strategies

Effective meal prep strategies can make staying committed to the carnivore diet much easier.

Learn How to Handle Cravings

Cravings can be a common challenge when following the carnivore diet, especially if transitioning from a diet that includes carbohydrates and sugars.

Dining Out Tips

Eating out while following a carnivore diet can be challenging, but with a few strategies, you can navigate restaurant menus and stay on track.

Staying Hydrated

Proper hydration is crucial for overall health and can help you stay on track with your carnivore diet.

Tracking Progress and Staying Motivated

Maintaining motivation and tracking your progress is essential for long-term success on the carnivore diet.

Scan the QR code to get your FREE ebook right now

The carnivore diet is a dietary approach that focuses exclusively on consuming animal-based foods while eliminating all plant-based foods. This diet consists of meat, fish, eggs, and, in some variations, dairy products. The central premise of the carnivore diet is that humans are optimized to thrive on a diet composed primarily of animal products, which proponents believe to be nutritionally complete and sufficient for maintaining health.

Those who follow the carnivore diet often enjoy a variety of meats, including beef, pork, lamb, and poultry. Fatty cuts of meat are particularly favored as they provide the necessary proteins and fats for energy and bodily functions. Fish and seafood, which are rich in omega-3 fatty acids and other essential nutrients, are also important components of the diet. Organ meats, such as liver, kidneys, and heart, are highly valued for their dense nutrient profiles, which contain vitamins and minerals that are critical for health.

Dairy products are included in some versions of the carnivore diet, although their inclusion depends on individual tolerance. Eggs, being versatile and nutrient-dense, are commonly consumed and provide a range of essential nutrients, including high-quality protein, vitamins, and minerals.

The carnivore diet, controversial in the nutrition community, excludes all plant-based foods, including fruits, vegetables, grains, nuts, seeds, legumes, and anything derived from plants. This exclusion is based on the belief that plant foods contain anti-nutrients and compounds that may interfere with nutrient absorption and cause digestive issues for some individuals. By eliminating these foods, the diet aims to avoid potential sources of inflammation and digestive discomfort, though this aspect of the diet is often debated within the broader nutrition community.

This dietary approach necessitates a significant shift in eating habits and meal planning. It involves preparing simple meals centered around animal products and using cooking methods that preserve the nutritional integrity of these foods, such as grilling, roasting, and frying with animal fats like tallow or lard. The diet also strongly emphasizes consuming water and, in some cases, bone broth to maintain hydration and support electrolyte balance, given that traditional sources of electrolytes from plant foods are not present.

Overall, the carnivore diet represents a radical departure from conventional nutritional advice, emphasizing a return to what its proponents argue is a more natural, ancestral way of eating. This diet requires a commitment to a particular set of food choices and eliminating a broad range of foods commonly consumed in modern diets. As such, it represents a lifestyle choice beyond mere dietary preference, involving a comprehensive rethinking of one's approach to food and nutrition.

The carnivore diet, characterized by its exclusive focus on animal-based foods, offers a range of potential benefits that attract many followers. Here are some of the key benefits:

Reduction in Inflammation: Adherents of the carnivore diet report a significant decrease in inflammation. By eliminating plant-based foods, which can contain antinutrients and inflammatory compounds, the diet aims to minimize sources of irritation within the body. This can benefit individuals with autoimmune conditions, arthritis, or chronic inflammatory diseases. The diet's emphasis on nutrient-dense animal products helps to support the body's natural anti-inflammatory processes.

Improved Digestion and Gut Health: Many people experience improved digestion when switching to a carnivore diet. Plant-based foods, mainly those high in fiber, can cause bloating, gas, and other digestive issues in some individuals. The carnivore diet can reduce digestive discomfort and promote better gut health by focusing solely on easily digestible animal products. This simplified diet allows the digestive system to function more efficiently, potentially alleviating irritable bowel syndrome (IBS) symptoms and other digestive disorders.

Enhanced Mental Clarity and Focus: The carnivore diet may also improve mental clarity and cognitive function. Supporters of the diet report experiencing fewer brain fog episodes and better overall mental performance. The diet's high fat and protein content provides a steady source of energy for the brain, helping to stabilize blood sugar levels and avoid the energy crashes that can occur with carbohydrate-heavy diets. This stable energy supply can improve concentration, mood stability, and cognitive performance.

Effective Weight Management: The carnivore diet can be an effective tool for managing weight. The diet's high protein and fat content promotes satiety, helping individuals feel fuller for extended periods and reducing the urge to snack between meals. This natural reduction in calorie intake can lead to weight loss without strict calorie counting or portion control. The diet's focus on whole, unprocessed foods can help maintain a healthier body composition.

Simplified Meal Planning: Another appealing aspect of the carnivore diet is its simplicity in meal planning and preparation. With a limited range of food choices, meal planning becomes straightforward and less time-consuming. This simplicity can make it easier for individuals to adhere to their dietary goals and maintain consistency. The diet eliminates the need for complex recipes and extensive grocery lists, allowing for a more streamlined and manageable approach to eating.

Increased Muscle Mass and Strength: The carnivore diet, rich in high-quality protein, is highly effective in supporting muscle growth and maintenance. Protein is essential for muscle repair and development, making this diet particularly beneficial for athletes and those engaged in regular physical activity.

Improved Skin Health: Many individuals on the carnivore diet report noticeable improvements in their skin health. Conditions like acne, eczema, and psoriasis may improve or even clear up entirely. The diet's high intake of collagen-rich foods like bone broth and organ meats can support skin elasticity and hydration.

Enhanced Satiety and Reduced Cravings: The carnivore diet's emphasis on protein and fat increases feelings of fullness and satiety, reducing the frequency and intensity of food cravings. This can be particularly beneficial for those struggling with overeating or addiction to sugary foods and snacks. By stabilizing blood sugar levels and providing steady energy, the diet helps to curb the desire for unhealthy foods, making it easier to maintain a balanced eating pattern.

Increased Energy Levels: Many followers of the carnivore diet experience a notable increase in energy levels. The diet's high fat and protein content provides a more stable and long-lasting energy source compared to carbohydrates, which can cause energy spikes and crashes.

Comprehensive Guide to Carnivore Diet Foods

The carnivore diet focuses exclusively on animal-based foods, eliminating all plant-based foods. Here's a detailed guide to the types of foods you can include in your carnivore diet:

Meat

Beef: The cornerstone of the carnivore diet, beef provides essential nutrients and is versatile. Popular cuts include ribeye, sirloin, ground beef, and brisket.

- Steak (rib eye, sirloin, filet mignon)
- Ground beef (for burgers, meatballs, and more)
- Roasts (chuck roast, brisket)
- Organ meats (liver, kidneys, heart)

Pork: Another staple, pork offers a range of options, from lean cuts to fatty pieces.

- Bacon
- Pork chops
- Pork belly
- Ham
- Sausages (ensure they are free from fillers and sugars)

Lamb: Rich in flavor and nutrients, lamb can add variety to your diet.

- Lamb chops
- Leg of lamb
- Lamb shank

Poultry: A good source of protein.

- Chicken
- Turkey
- Duck

Game Meat: For those seeking variety and unique flavors, game meats are excellent options.

- Venison (deer)
- Bison
- Elk
- Rabbit

Fish and Seafood: Rich in omega-3 fatty acids and protein, fish is a valuable addition.

- Salmon
- Tuna
- Sardines
- Mackerel
- Cod

Shellfish: Shellfish are high in nutrients like zinc and vitamin B12.

- Shrimp
- Lobster
- Crab
- Mussels
- Oysters

Eggs: Eggs are nutrient-dense and versatile.

- Chicken eggs
- Duck eggs
- Quail eggs

Dairy (If Tolerated): Some people on the carnivore diet include dairy products, though individual tolerance varies.

- Butter
- Heavy cream
- Cheese (cheddar, mozzarella, gouda)
- Yogurt (unsweetened, full-fat)

Fats: Healthy fats are an essential part of the carnivore diet.

- Animal fats (beef tallow, lard, duck fat)
- Butter and ghee
- Bone marrow

Organ Meats: Organ meats are nutrient powerhouses, offering vitamins and minerals not found in muscle meats.

- Liver
- Kidneys
- Heart
- Brain
- Sweetbreads

Bone Broth: Bone broth is rich in collagen, amino acids, and minerals.

- Homemade bone broth (made from beef, chicken, or pork bones)

Tips for Selecting Carnivore Diet Foods

- **Opt for Grass-Fed and Pasture-Raised:** Choose grass-fed beef and pasture-raised animals for higher nutrient content and better fat profiles.

- **Read Labels:** For processed meats like bacon and sausages, ensure they do not contain added sugars, fillers, or artificial additives.

- **Experiment with Different Cuts:** Explore various cuts of meat to keep your diet exciting and satisfying.

- **Balance Fat and Protein:** Ensure you're consuming enough fats to feel satiated, especially when eating leaner cuts of meat.

- **Include Organ Meats:** Incorporate organ meats regularly to benefit from their unique nutrient profiles.

- **Hydrate and Supplement:** Drink plenty of water and consider supplementing with electrolytes to maintain balance, especially during the initial adaptation phase.

Temperature Guides and Meat Quality for the Carnivore Diet

Proper preparation and high-quality meat are essential components of the carnivore diet. Here's a detailed guide to cooking temperatures and selecting the best meat quality.

Cooking Temperature Guide

Beef:

- Rare: 120-125°F (49-52°C)
- Medium Rare: 130-135°F (54-57°C)
- Medium: 140-145°F (60-63°C)
- Medium Well: 150-155°F (65-68°C)
- Well Done: 160°F+ (71°C+)

Pork:

- Medium Rare: 145°F (63°C) (minimum safe internal temperature)
- Medium: 150°F (66°C)
- Medium Well: 155°F (68°C)
- Well Done: 160°F+ (71°C+)

Lamb:

- Rare: 125°F (52°C)
- Medium Rare: 130-135°F (54-57°C)
- Medium: 140-145°F (60-63°C)
- Medium Well: 150-155°F (65-68°C)
- Well Done: 160°F+ (71°C+)

Poultry:

- Chicken or Turkey Breast: 165°F (74°C)
- Chicken or Turkey Thighs/Wings: 165°F (74°C)

Fish:

- Well Done: 140°F+ (60°C+)

Ground Meat:

- Beef, Pork, Lamb, Veal: 160°F (71°C)
- Poultry: 165°F (74°C)

Tips for Achieving Perfect Cooking Temperatures

- **Use a Meat Thermometer:** To ensure accuracy, always use a digital meat thermometer to check internal temperatures.

- **Rest Meat:** After cooking, let the meat rest for a few minutes to allow the juices to redistribute, which helps maintain moisture and flavor.

- **Carryover Cooking:** Remember that meat continues to cook slightly after being removed from the heat, so it's a good idea to take it off the heat a few degrees below your target temperature.

Selecting High-Quality Meat

Beef:

- **Grass-Fed vs. Grain-Fed:** Grass-fed beef is often richer in nutrients, such as omega-3 fatty acids and conjugated linoleic acid (CLA), and is of higher quality.

- **Marbling:** Look for good marbling (intramuscular fat) in cuts like ribeye and sirloin, as this adds flavor and tenderness.

- **Organic:** Opt for organic beef to avoid exposure to hormones and antibiotics.

Pork:

- **Pasture-Raised:** Choose pasture-raised pork for better flavor and nutritional content.

- **Color:** High-quality pork should have a pinkish-red color and some marbling.

Lamb:

- **Grass-Fed:** Like beef, grass-fed lamb is preferable for its nutrient profile.

- **Freshness:** Ensure the meat is fresh, with a bright red color and no off odors.

Poultry:

- **Free-Range/Organic:** Free-range or organic poultry is typically raised in better conditions and is free from antibiotics and hormones.

- **Skin and Fat:** Look for birds with healthy, unblemished skin and a good amount of fat.

Fish and Seafood:

- **Wild-Caught vs. Farmed:** Wild-caught fish generally have higher nutritional value and fewer contaminants than farmed fish.

- **Freshness:** Ensure fish has bright, clear eyes, shiny skin, and a fresh ocean smell. Avoid fish that looks dull or has a strong fishy odor.

Eggs:

- **Pasture-Raised:** These eggs come from chickens that can roam freely, leading to higher omega-3 content and better overall nutrition.

- **Organic:** Organic eggs are produced without synthetic pesticides or fertilizers, ensuring a cleaner product.

Dairy (If Tolerated)

- **Grass-Fed:** Grass-fed dairy products have higher omega-3 fatty acids and CLA levels.

- **Raw vs. Pasteurized:** Some people on the carnivore diet prefer raw dairy for its enzymes and beneficial bacteria, but it should come from a trusted source to ensure safety.

Additional Tips for Meat Quality

- **Local Sourcing:** Whenever possible, buy meat from local farmers or butchers who can provide information about the sourcing and quality of their products.

- **Avoid Processed Meats:** Avoid processed meats that contain additives, preservatives, and fillers. Opt for whole cuts of meat instead.

- **Proper Storage:** Store meat properly to maintain its quality. Keep refrigerated and use or freeze it within recommended time frames to prevent spoilage.

- **Consider Buying in Bulk:** For cost savings and convenience, consider buying meat in bulk and freezing portions for later use.

By following these guidelines on cooking temperatures and selecting high-quality meats, you can ensure that your carnivore diet is safe and nutritious.

Meal Plan

Day	Breakfast	Lunch	Snack	Dinner
1	Bacon and Eggs P- 13	Ribeye Steak p- 23	Fried Calamari Rings p -44	Bacon-Wrapped Pork Tenderloin p -39
2	Egg and Chicken sausage Casserole P-13	Butter Lamb Chops p - 24	Garlic Butter Grilled Prawns p -48	Grilled Salmon Fillets p -40
3	Egg and Duck Sausage Skillet P-14	Pork Spare Ribs p - 29	Bacon Wrapped Shrimp p -49	Garlic Butter Clams p -44
4	Cheese Omelette P- 14	Beef Chuck Roast p - 31	Smoked Salmon Deviled Eggs p -49	Grilled Shrimp and Scallop Skewers p -47
5	Venison Breakfast Sausage P -15	Roasted Lamb Racks p - 34	Chicken Wings p -51	Grilled Chicken Thighs p -50
6	Duck Eggs and Steak for Two P- 15	Beef Sausages p -36	Chicken Hearts Skewers p -54	Grilled Chicken Breast p -53
7	Fried Pork Belly p-16	Seekh Kebab p - 30	Turkey Bacon Strips p -56	Turkey Breast Cutlets p -59
8	Scrambled Eggs with Ham p-16	Bacon-Wrapped Filet Mignon p -23	Grilled Chicken Skewers p -57	Carnivore Turkey Burgers p -54
9	Poached Eggs p- 17	Homemade Deli-Style Roast Beef p- 28	Turkey Meatballs p -57	Chicken Thighs with Lemon Pepper p -58

Day	Breakfast	Lunch	Snack	Dinner
10	Chorizo and Eggs p- 17	Homemade Bacon p -25	Turkey Sausages p -58	Broiled Lobster Tails p -42
11	Salmon and Eggs p -18	Braised Lamb Shank p -27	Duck Fat Fried Chicken Wings p -59	Shrimp Scampi p -41
12	Bison and Egg Muffins p -18	Beef Ribs p -35	Chicken Liver Sauté p -60	Grilled Octopus Tentacles p -45
13	Carnivore Scotch Eggs p -19	Beef Short Ribs p - 29	Roast Chicken Drumsticks p -60	Lemon Pepper Grilled Salmon p -47
14	Bacon-Wrapped Egg Cups p -20	Grilled Beef Heart p -24	Chicken Bone Broth p -61	Roast Chicken with Herb Butter p -50
15	Egg and Ham Omelette p- 20	Beef Meatballs p -30	Shredded Chicken p -62	Pan-Seared Duck Breast p -51
16	Bacon-Wrapped Smokies p - 21	Lamb Brain Fritters p -25	Crispy Smoked Chicken Wings p -62	Bacon Wrapped Cod p -48
17	Carnivore Beef Liver Pancakes p -22	Venison Tenderloin p - 31	Salt and Vinegar Wings p -63	Roasted Turkey Drumsticks p -52
18	Bacon and Eggs P- 13	Beef Brisket p -28	Carnivore Fried Chicken p -63	Roast Duck p -55

Day	Breakfast	Lunch	Snack	Dinner
19	Egg and Chicken sausage Casserole P-13	Classic Organ Meat Pie p -38	Homemade Pork Rinds p- 37	Baked Cod with Lemon Butter p -41
20	Egg and Duck Sausage Skillet P-14	Pork Tenderloin p -26	Chicken Meatballs p -65	Steamed Crab Legs with Drawn Butter p- 43
21	Cheese Omelette P- 14	Pork Loin Roast p -35	Chicken Skin Chips p -65	Carnivore Crab Cakes p -46
22	Venison Breakfast Sausage P -15	Bacon-Wrapped Pork Chops p -37	Bacon-Wrapped Chicken Sausages p -66	Smoked Turkey Legs p -55
23	Duck Eggs and Steak for Two P- 15	Pork Patties p- 36	Carnivore Nuggets p -67	Bacon-Wrapped Pan-Seared Scallops p -45
24	Fried Pork Belly p-16	Bacon-Wrapped Steak p - 32	Fried Pork Belly p -16	Chicken Burger Patties p -52
25	Scrambled Eggs with Ham p-16	T-Bone Steak p - 26	Bacon-Wrapped Smokies p -21	Seared Scallops with Garlic Butter p -42
26	Poached Eggs p- 17	Roast Leg of Lamb p - 33	Homemade Bacon p -25	Duck Confit p -53
27	Chorizo and Eggs p- 17	Carnivore Pizza p -38	Seekh Kebab p -30	Roast Quail p -56

Day	Breakfast	Lunch	Snack	Dinner
28	Salmon and Eggs p -18	Ground Beef Patties p -27	Beef Meatballs p -30	Pan-Seared Tuna Steaks p -40
29	Bison and Egg Muffins p -18	Bison Chuck Roast p -34	Bacon-Wrapped Spam Bites p -32	Grilled Sardines p -46
30	Carnivore Scotch Eggs p -19	Lamb Kabobs p - 33	Lamb Kabobs p -33	Blackened Catfish Fillets p -43

Bacon and Eggs

Ingredients

- 4 slices of bacon
- 2 large eggs
- Salt and pepper to taste

Instructions

Cook 4 bacon slices in a skillet until crispy, then remove. In the same skillet, cook 2 eggs to your preferred doneness. Season with salt and pepper. Serve the eggs with the bacon. Enjoy!

Servings-1, Total cooking time - 15 mins
Kcal- 400, Proteins- 20g, Fats- 35g, Carbs- 1g

Egg and Chicken Sausage Casserole

Ingredients

- 1 lb chicken sausage, sliced or crumbled
- 8 large eggs
- Salt and pepper to taste

Instructions

Preheat your oven to 375°F (190°C). Over medium heat, cook 1 lb of chicken sausage in a skillet until browned and cooked through. Whisk together 8 eggs, salt, and pepper in a large bowl. Grease a baking dish and spread the cooked sausage evenly on the bottom. Pour the egg mixture over the sausage. Bake in the oven for 25-30 minutes until the eggs are fully set and the top is golden brown. Let the casserole cool slightly before slicing and serving.

Servings-5, Total cooking time - 40 mins
Kcal- 350, Proteins- 25g, Fats- 25g, Carbs- 1g

Egg and Duck Sausage Skillet

Ingredients

- 1/2 lb duck sausage, sliced or crumbled
- 4 large eggs
- Salt and pepper to taste

Instructions

Heat a skillet over medium heat. Add 1/2 lb of duck sausage until browned and cooked, about 5-7 minutes. Crack 4 eggs into the skillet with the sausage. Cook the eggs to your preferred doneness—season with salt and pepper to taste. Serve immediately.

**Servings-2, Total cooking time - 15 mins
Kcal- 450, Proteins- 30g, Fats- 35g, Carbs- 1g**

Cheese Omelette

Ingredients

- 3 large eggs
- 1/4 cup shredded cheese (cheddar, Swiss, or your choice)
- 1 tbsp butter
- Salt and pepper to taste

Instructions

Whisk 3 eggs with salt and pepper—heat 1 tbsp of butter in a non-stick skillet over medium heat until melted. Pour in the eggs and cook for 1-2 minutes. Sprinkle 1/4 cup of shredded cheese on one half, fold the omelette, and cook for another 1-2 minutes until the cheese melts. Serve immediately.

**Servings-1, Total cooking time - 10 mins
Kcal- 300, Proteins- 20g, Fats- 25g, Carbs- 1g**

Ingredients

- 2 pounds ground venison
- 1 pound ground pork (optional for added fat)
- 2 teaspoons salt
- Optional:1 teaspoon black pepper,1 teaspoon garlic powder, 1 teaspoon onion powder, 1 teaspoon dried sage, 1 teaspoon dried thyme, 1/2 teaspoon crushed red pepper flakes, 1/2 teaspoon fennel seeds

Instructions

In a large bowl, mix the venison, pork (if using), salt, pepper, garlic powder, onion powder, sage, thyme, red pepper flakes, and fennel seeds (if using). Form it into patties or keep it loose. Cook in a skillet over medium heat for 4-5 minutes per side for patties or until browned and fully cooked if loose. Serve hot.

**Servings-12, Total cooking time - 20 mins
Kcal- 150, Proteins- 18g, Fats- 9g, Carbs- 1g**

Ingredients

- 2 duck eggs
- 2 (6-8 ounce) steaks (ribeye or sirloin)
- 2 tablespoons butter or tallow
- Salt and pepper to taste
- Optional: 1 teaspoon garlic powder, 1 teaspoon onion powder, Fresh herbs (such as thyme or rosemary)

Instructions

Season steaks with salt, pepper, garlic powder, and onion powder (if using). Heat one tablespoon of butter in a skillet over medium-high heat. Cook steaks for 4-5 minutes per side for medium-rare, then let rest. In the same skillet, add the remaining butter and reduce heat to medium. Crack duck eggs into the skillet and cook for 3-4 minutes until the whites are set. Serve each steak with a fried duck egg on top, garnished with herbs if desired.

**Servings-2, Total cooking time - 15 mins
Kcal- 650, Proteins- 50g, Fats- 50g, Carbs- 1g**

Fried Pork Belly

Ingredients

- 1 pound pork belly, sliced into 1/2-inch thick pieces
- Salt to taste

Instructions

Season the pork belly slices with salt. Heat a large skillet over medium-high heat. Add the pork belly slices in a single layer. Cook for 4-5 minutes on each side until crispy and golden brown. Remove from the skillet and drain on paper towels. Serve hot.

Servings-2, Total cooking time - 15 mins
Kcal- 600, Proteins- 12g, Fats- 60g, Carbs- 0g

Scrambled Eggs with Ham

Ingredients

- 4 large eggs
- 1/2 cup diced ham
- 1 tablespoon butter
- Salt and pepper to taste
- Fresh chives or parsley (optional, for garnish)

Instructions

Whisk the eggs with a pinch of salt and pepper in a bowl. Heat the butter in a skillet over medium heat. Add the diced ham and cook for 2-3 minutes until lightly browned. Pour in the eggs and stir gently until set, about 2-3 minutes. Serve hot, garnished with fresh chives or parsley if desired.

Servings-2, Total cooking time - 10 mins
Kcal- 220, Proteins- 18g, Fats- 16g, Carbs- 1g

Poached Eggs

Ingredients

- 4 large eggs
- 2 tablespoons vinegar (optional)
- Salt to taste

Instructions

Fill a large saucepan with water and bring it to a gentle simmer over medium heat. Add the vinegar if using. Crack each egg into a small bowl. With a spoon, create a gentle whirlpool in the simmering water and carefully slide one egg into the center. Poach for 3-4 minutes until the whites are set, but the yolks are still runny. Remove with a slotted spoon and drain on paper towels. Repeat with the remaining eggs. Serve hot, seasoned with salt.

Servings-2, Total cooking time - 10 mins
Kcal- 150, Proteins- 10g, Fats- 12g, Carbs- 1g

Chorizo and Eggs

Ingredients

- 4 large eggs
- 1/2 pound chorizo sausage, casing removed
- 1 tablespoon butter or tallow
- Salt and pepper to taste

Instructions

Heat butter or tallow in a skillet over medium heat. Add the chorizo and cook, breaking it up with a spoon, until browned and cooked through, about 5-6 minutes. In a bowl, whisk the eggs with a pinch of salt and pepper. Pour the eggs into the skillet with the chorizo and cook, stirring gently, until the eggs are just set, about 2-3 minutes. Serve hot.

Servings-2, Total cooking time - 10 mins
Kcal- 400, Proteins- 25g, Fats- 32g, Carbs- 1g

Salmon and Eggs

Ingredients

- 4 large eggs
- 1/2 pound salmon fillet, skin removed, cut into small pieces
- 1 tablespoon butter
- Salt and pepper to taste

Instructions

In a bowl, whisk the eggs with a pinch of salt and pepper. Heat the butter in a skillet over medium heat. Add the salmon pieces and cook for 3-4 minutes until cooked. Pour the eggs into the skillet with the salmon and cook, stirring gently, until the eggs are just set, about 2-3 minutes. Serve hot.

Servings-2, Total cooking time - 10 mins
Kcal- 300, Proteins- 25g, Fats- 20g, Carbs- 1g

Bison and Egg Muffins

Ingredients

- 1/2 pound ground bison
- 4 large eggs
- Salt and pepper to taste
- 1 tablespoon butter or tallow
- Optional: 1/2 teaspoon garlic powder, 1/2 teaspoon onion powder

Instructions

Preheat your oven to 350°F (175°C) and grease a muffin tin with butter or fat. In a skillet, cook the ground bison over medium heat until browned, seasoning with salt, pepper, garlic powder, and onion powder if using. In a bowl, whisk the eggs with a pinch of salt and pepper. Divide the cooked bison evenly into the muffin tin cups. Pour the whisked eggs over the bison, filling each cup. Bake for 15-18 minutes or until the eggs are set. Let cool slightly before removing from the tin. Serve hot.

Servings-2, Total cooking time - 25 mins
Kcal- 300, Proteins- 28g, Fats- 20g, Carbs- 1g

Chicken Liver Pâté

Ingredients

- 1 pound chicken livers, trimmed
- 1/2 cup butter or tallow
- 2 cloves garlic, minced
- Salt and pepper to taste
- Optional: 1 teaspoon dried thyme, 1/4 cup chicken broth

Instructions

Heat 1/4 cup of butter or fat in a large skillet over medium heat. Add the garlic and cook for a minute. Add the chicken livers to the skillet and cook until they are no longer pink in the center, about 5-7 minutes. Season with salt, pepper, and thyme if using. Transfer the mixture to a food processor and blend until smooth, adding the remaining butter or fat and chicken broth (if using) to reach the desired consistency. Taste and adjust seasoning if needed. Transfer the pâté to a dish and chill in the refrigerator for at least 1 hour before serving.

Servings-4, Total cooking time - 20 mins
Kcal- 250, Proteins- 18g, Fats- 20g, Carbs- 1g

Carnivore Scotch Eggs

Ingredients

- 4 large eggs
- 1 pound ground pork (or ground beef, bison, or lamb)
- 1 teaspoon salt
- 1 tablespoon butter or tallow
- 1/2 teaspoon black pepper
- Optional: 1/2 teaspoon garlic powder, 1/2 teaspoon onion powder

Instructions

Boil the eggs for 6 minutes, then cool in an ice bath and peel. Mix ground meat with salt, pepper, garlic powder, and onion powder. Divide into four portions, flatten, and wrap each around an egg. Heat butter or tallow in a skillet over medium heat and cook the wrapped eggs, turning occasionally, until the meat is browned and cooked through, about 10-12 minutes. Serve hot.

Servings-2, Total cooking time - 30 mins
Kcal- 550, Proteins- 40g, Fats- 40g, Carbs- 2g

<table>
<tr><td>

Ingredients

- 6 large eggs
- 6 slices of bacon
- Salt and pepper to taste
- Optional: 1/2 teaspoon garlic powder, 1/2 teaspoon onion powder

Instructions

Preheat your oven to 375°F (190°C). Grease a muffin tin with a bit of butter or tallow. Partially cook the bacon slices in a skillet over medium heat until they begin to brown but are still pliable about 3-4 minutes. Line each muffin cup with a bacon slice, forming a ring around the edges. Crack an egg into each bacon-lined cup. Season with salt, pepper, garlic powder, and onion powder if using. Bake in the oven for 12-15 minutes or until the egg whites are set to your liking. Remove from the oven and cool slightly before removing the egg cups from the tin. Serve hot.

Servings-3, Total cooking time - 25 mins
Kcal- 250, Proteins- 15g, Fats- 20g, Carbs- 1g

</td><td>

Ingredients

- 4 large eggs
- 1/2 cup diced ham
- 1 tablespoon butter
- Salt and pepper to taste
- Optional: 1/2 teaspoon garlic powder, 1/2 teaspoon onion powder

Instructions

In a bowl, whisk the eggs with a pinch of salt, pepper, garlic powder, and onion powder—heat butter in a skillet over medium heat. Add the diced ham and cook for 2-3 minutes until lightly browned. Pour the eggs into the skillet, swirling to coat the bottom evenly. Cook without stirring for 2-3 minutes until the eggs start to set. Gently lift the edges of the omelette with a spatula, allowing any uncooked egg to flow underneath. Once the omelette is almost set, fold it in half and cook for another minute. Serve hot.

Servings-2, Total cooking time - 10 mins
Kcal- 250, Proteins- 20g, Fats- 18g, Carbs- 1g

</td></tr>
</table>

Bacon-Wrapped Smokies

Ingredients

- 1 pound little smokies sausages
- 12 slices of bacon, cut into thirds

Instructions

Preheat your oven to 375°F (190°C). Wrap each little smokie with a piece of bacon and secure it with a toothpick. Arrange the bacon-wrapped smokies on a baking sheet lined with parchment paper. Bake in the oven for 20-25 minutes or until the bacon is crispy. Remove from the oven and let rest for a few minutes before serving. Serve hot.

Servings-8, Total cooking time -30 mins Kcal- 230, Proteins- 12g, Fats- 20g, Carbs- 1g

Bacon Mayo

Ingredients

- 4 slices of bacon
- 1 large egg yolk
- 1 teaspoon Dijon mustard
- 1 teaspoon lemon juice
- 1/2 cup bacon fat (from cooked bacon), cooled but still liquid
- Salt and pepper to taste

Instructions

Cook the bacon in a skillet over medium heat until crispy. Remove the bacon and set aside, reserving the bacon fat. Let the bacon fat cool slightly but remain liquid. Whisk together the egg yolk, Dijon mustard, and lemon juice in a bowl until well combined. Slowly drizzle in the bacon fat while continuously whisking until the mixture thickens and emulsifies into mayonnaise. Crumble the cooked bacon and fold it into the mayonnaise— season with salt and pepper to taste. Store in the refrigerator until ready to use.

Servings-1 cup Total cooking time - 15 mins Kcal- 100, Proteins- 1g, Fats- 11g, Carbs- 0g

Egg White Wraps

Ingredients

- 4 large egg whites
- 1 tablespoon butter
- Salt and pepper to taste

Instructions

Whisk the egg whites in a bowl with a pinch of salt and pepper until frothy. Heat a non-stick skillet over medium heat and add the butter. Pour a portion of the egg whites, tilting the skillet to spread them evenly into a thin layer, similar to making a crepe. Cook for 1-2 minutes or until the edges lift and the bottom is set. Carefully flip the wrap and cook for another 1-2 minutes until fully cooked. Remove from the skillet and repeat with the remaining egg whites. Serve hot with your favorite fillings or use as a wrap for other ingredients.

Servings-2, Total cooking time - 10 mins
Kcal- 34, Proteins- 7g, Fats- 2g, Carbs- 0g

Carnivore Beef Liver Pancakes

Ingredients

- 1/2 pound beef liver, cut into pieces
- 2 large eggs
- 1/4 cup pork rinds, crushed into a fine powder
- 2 tablespoons heavy cream (optional)
- Salt to taste
- Optional: 1 teaspoon garlic powder, 1 teaspoon onion powder

Instructions

Blend beef liver until smooth. Whisk eggs and cream, then mix pork rinds, salt, garlic, and onion powder into the liver. Heat butter or tallow in a skillet over medium heat. Pour 1/4 cup batter into the skillet to form a pancake, and cook 2-3 minutes per side until browned. Repeat and serve hot.

Servings-4, Total cooking time - 20 mins
Kcal- 200, Proteins- 20g, Fats- 12g, Carbs- 1g

Ribeye Steak

Ingredients

- 2 (10-12 ounce) ribeye steaks
- 2 tablespoons butter or tallow
- Salt and pepper to taste
- Optional: 1 teaspoon garlic powder, 1 teaspoon onion powder

Instructions

Season the ribeye steaks generously with salt, pepper, garlic powder, and onion powder—heat butter or tallow in a skillet over high heat until hot. Add the steaks and sear for 3-4 minutes on each side for medium-rare, or adjust the time according to your preferred level of doneness. For thicker steaks, reduce heat to medium after searing and cook for 2-3 minutes per side. Remove the steaks from the skillet and let them rest for 5 minutes before serving. Serve hot.

Servings-2, Total cooking time - 15 mins
Kcal- 650, Proteins- 45g, Fats- 50g, Carbs- 0g

Bacon-Wrapped Filet Mignon

Ingredients

- 2 (6-8 ounce) filet mignon steaks
- 2 slices of bacon
- 1 tablespoon butter or tallow
- Salt and pepper to taste
- Optional: 1 teaspoon garlic powder, 1 teaspoon onion powder

Instructions

Preheat oven to 400°F (200°C). Wrap each filet mignon with bacon and secure it with twine—season with salt, pepper, garlic, and onion powder. Sear in butter or tallow for 2-3 minutes per side, then bake in the oven for 5-7 minutes for medium-rare. Let rest for 5 minutes before serving.

Servings-2, Total cooking time - 20 mins
Kcal- 500, Proteins- 40g, Fats- 35g, Carbs- 1g

Ingredients

- 4 lamb chops
- 2 tablespoons butter
- Salt and pepper to taste
- Optional: 1 teaspoon garlic powder, 1 teaspoon onion powder, fresh rosemary or thyme for garnish

Instructions

Season the lamb chops generously with salt, pepper, garlic powder, and onion powder if using. Heat a skillet over medium-high heat. Add the butter and let it melt. Once the butter is hot and bubbling, add the lamb chops. Cook for 3-4 minutes on each side until they reach your desired level of doneness. Remove the lamb chops from the skillet and let them rest for a few minutes. Garnish with fresh rosemary or thyme if desired and serve hot.

Servings-2, Total cooking time - 10 mins
Kcal- 400, Proteins- 25g, Fats- 35g, Carbs- 1g

Ingredients

- 1 beef heart, cleaned and trimmed
- 3 tablespoons butter or tallow
- Salt and pepper to taste
- Optional: 1 teaspoon garlic powder, 1 teaspoon onion powder, 1 teaspoon smoked paprika

Instructions

Slice the beef heart into 1/2-inch thick strips. In a bowl, mix butter, salt, pepper, garlic powder, onion powder, and smoked paprika. Add the beef heart strips to the bowl and coat them with the seasoning mixture. Preheat your grill to medium-high heat. Grill the beef heart strips on each side for 3-4 minutes until they are nicely charred and cooked to your desired level of doneness. Remove from the grill and let rest for a few minutes before serving. Serve hot.

Servings-4, Total cooking time - 20 mins
Kcal- 250, Proteins- 28g, Fats- 15g, Carbs- 1g

Homemade Bacon

Ingredients

- 1 pork belly slab (about 2-3 pounds)
- 1/4 cup sea salt
- 2 tablespoons black pepper
- Optional: 1 tablespoon garlic powder, 1 tablespoon onion powder, 1 tablespoon smoked paprika

Instructions

Rinse and pat dry the pork belly. Rub with a mix of salt, pepper, garlic, onion powder, and smoked paprika. Refrigerate for 5-7 days, turning daily. After curing, rinse and dry. Preheat the smoker to 200°F (93°C) and smoke for 3-4 hours until the internal temperature reaches 150°F (65°C). Cool, refrigerate, slice, and cook in a skillet until crispy, 2-3 minutes per side. Serve hot.

Servings-7, Total cooking time - 7 days
Kcal- 300, Proteins- 15g, Fats- 25g, Carbs- 1g

Lamb Brain Fritters

Ingredients

- 1 pound lamb brains, cleaned
- 2 large eggs
- 1/2 cup pork rinds, crushed (or pork rind flour)
- Salt and pepper to taste
- 2 tablespoons butter or tallow

Instructions

Gently boil the lamb brains in salted water for 5 minutes. Remove, drain, and let cool. Once cooled, cut the brains into small pieces. In a bowl, beat the eggs and season with salt and pepper. Place the crushed pork rinds in another bowl. Heat butter or tallow in a skillet over medium heat. Dip each piece of lamb brain into the beaten eggs, then coat with the crushed pork rinds. Fry the coated brain pieces in the hot oil for 2-3 minutes on each side until golden and crispy. Remove from the skillet and drain on paper towels. Serve hot.

Servings-4, Total cooking time - 20 mins
Kcal- 250, Proteins- 15g, Fats- 20g, Carbs- 1g

Pork Tenderloin

Ingredients

- 1 pork tenderloin (about 1 pound)
- 2 tablespoons butter or tallow
- Salt and pepper to taste
- Optional: 1 teaspoon garlic powder, 1 teaspoon onion powder, 1 teaspoon smoked paprika

Instructions

Preheat your oven to 400°F (200°C). Season the pork tenderloin generously with salt, pepper, garlic powder, onion powder, and smoked paprika if using— heat butter or tallow in an oven-safe skillet over medium-high heat. Sear the tenderloin on all sides until browned, about 2-3 minutes per side. Transfer the skillet to the preheated oven and roast for 15-20 minutes or until the internal temperature reaches 145°F (63°C). Remove from the oven and let rest for 5 minutes before slicing. Serve hot.

Servings-2, Total cooking time - 30 mins
Kcal- 250, Proteins- 30g, Fats- 12g, Carbs- 1g

T-Bone Steak

Ingredients

- 2 T-bone steaks (about 1 inch thick)
- 2 tablespoons butter or tallow
- Salt and pepper to taste
- Optional: 1 teaspoon garlic powder, 1 teaspoon onion powder, fresh rosemary or thyme for garnish

Instructions

Season the T-bone steaks generously with salt, pepper, garlic powder, and onion powder if using. Heat butter or tallow in a large skillet over high heat until hot. Add the steaks and sear for 4-5 minutes on each side for medium-rare, or adjust the time according to your preferred level of doneness. For thicker steaks, reduce heat to medium after searing and cook for 2-3 minutes per side. Remove the steaks from the skillet and let them rest for 5 minutes before serving. Garnish with fresh rosemary or thyme if desired. Serve hot.

Servings-2, Total cooking time - 15 mins
Kcal- 700, Proteins- 45g, Fats- 55g, Carbs- 1g

Ground Beef Patties

Ingredients

- 1 pound ground beef (preferably 80/20 blend)
- Salt and pepper to taste
- Optional: 1 teaspoon garlic powder, 1 teaspoon onion powder

Instructions

Combine the ground beef in a bowl with salt, pepper, garlic powder, and onion powder if using. Mix until well combined. Divide the mixture into 4 equal portions and shape each into a patty. Heat a skillet or grill over medium-high heat. Cook the patties for 3-4 minutes on each side for medium-rare or until they reach your desired level of doneness. Remove from the skillet or grill and rest for a few minutes before serving. Serve hot.

Servings-2, Total cooking time - 15 mins
Kcal- 400, Proteins- 25g, Fats- 30g, Carbs- 1g

Braised Lamb Shank

Ingredients

- 2 lamb shanks
- 2 tablespoons butter or tallow
- Salt and pepper to taste
- Optional: 1 teaspoon garlic powder, 1 teaspoon onion powder, 1 teaspoon dried rosemary

Instructions

Preheat oven to 325°F (165°C). Season lamb shanks with salt, pepper, garlic, onion powder, and rosemary. Sear in butter or tallow until browned, 4-5 minutes per side. Add water or broth to cover halfway, simmer, cover, and braise in the oven for 2.5-3 hours until tender. Let rest before serving.

Servings-2, Total cooking time - 3 hrs 15 mins
Kcal- 450, Proteins- 40g, Fats- 30g, Carbs- 1g

Ingredients

- 3-4 pounds beef brisket
- 2 tablespoons butter or tallow
- Salt and pepper to taste
- Optional: 2 teaspoons garlic powder, 2 teaspoons onion powder, 1 teaspoon smoked paprika

Instructions

Preheat the oven to 300°F (150°C). Season the brisket with salt, pepper, garlic, onion powder, and smoked paprika. Sear in butter or tallow until browned, 4-5 minutes per side. Return the brisket to the pot, add water or broth to cover halfway, and bring to a simmer. Cover and cook in the oven for 3-4 hours until tender. Rest for 15 minutes before slicing. Serve hot.

Servings-6, Total cooking time - 4 hrs 30 mins
Kcal- 450, Proteins- 40g, Fats- 30g, Carbs- 1g

Ingredients

- 2-3 pound beef eye of round roast
- 2 tablespoons butter
- 1 teaspoon salt
- Optional: 1 teaspoon black pepper, 1 teaspoon garlic powder, 1 teaspoon onion powder, 1 teaspoon dried thyme

Instructions

Preheat your oven to 325°F (165°C). Rub the beef roast with butter, then season with salt, pepper, garlic powder, onion powder, and dried thyme if using. Place the roast on a rack in a roasting pan. Roast in the preheated oven until the internal temperature reaches 135°F (57°C) for about 1.5-2 hours for medium-rare. Remove the roast from the oven and let it rest for at least 15 minutes before slicing thinly against the grain. Serve hot or cold.

Servings-7, Total cooking time - 2 hrs 15 mins
Kcal- 250, Proteins- 25g, Fats- 15g, Carbs- 1g

Ingredients

- 2 racks of pork spare ribs (about 4-5 pounds)
- 3 tablespoons butter or tallow
- Salt and pepper to taste
- Optional: 2 teaspoons garlic powder, 2 teaspoons onion powder, 2 teaspoons smoked paprika

Instructions

Preheat the oven to 300°F (150°C). Season the pork spare ribs with salt, pepper, garlic, onion powder, and smoked paprika. Place them on a foil-lined baking sheet, drizzle with butter or tallow, and cover with foil. Bake for 2.5-3 hours until tender. Uncover, raise the oven to 400°F (200°C), and bake for 15-20 minutes to crisp. Let them rest before slicing. Serve hot.

Servings-5, Total cooking time - 3 hrs 30 mins Kcal- 600, Proteins- 40g, Fats- 45g, Carbs- 1g

Ingredients

- 4-6 beef short ribs
- 2 tablespoons butter or tallow
- Salt and pepper to taste
- Optional: 2 teaspoons garlic powder, 2 teaspoons onion powder, 1 teaspoon smoked paprika

Instructions

Preheat the oven to 325°F (165°C). Season the beef short ribs with salt, pepper, garlic, onion powder, and smoked paprika. Sear in butter or tallow for 3-4 minutes per side. Add water or broth to cover halfway, simmer, cover, and braise in the oven for 2.5-3 hours until tender. Let rest before serving. Serve hot.

Servings-4, Total cooking time - 3 hrs 30 mins Kcal- 600, Proteins- 40g, Fats- 45g, Carbs- 2g

Seekh Kebab

Ingredients

- 1 pound ground beef or lamb (80/20)
- 2 tablespoons finely minced fat
- 1 teaspoon salt
- 1/2 teaspoon black pepper
- Optional: 1/2 teaspoon smoked paprika, 1 teaspoon garlic powder, 1 teaspoon onion powder

Instructions

Combine the ground meat, minced fat, salt, black pepper, garlic powder, onion powder, and smoked paprika in a bowl. Mix until well combined. Divide the mixture into 4-6 portions and shape each into long, cylindrical kebabs around metal skewers. Preheat a grill or grill pan over medium-high heat. Grill the kebabs for 8-10 minutes, turning occasionally, until they are cooked and have a nice char. Remove from the grill and let rest for a few minutes before serving. Serve hot.

Servings-2, Total cooking time - 20 mins
Kcal- 350, Proteins- 20g, Fats- 28g, Carbs- 1g

Beef Meatballs

Ingredients

- 1 pound ground beef (80/20)
- 1/4 cup finely minced beef fat
- 1 teaspoon salt
- 1/2 teaspoon black pepper
- Optional: 1 teaspoon garlic powder, 1 teaspoon onion powder

Instructions

Preheat your oven to 375°F (190°C). Combine the ground beef, minced fat, salt, black pepper, garlic powder, and onion powder if using in a bowl. Mix until well combined. Form the mixture into 12-15 meatballs, about 1.5 inches in diameter each. Place the meatballs on a baking sheet lined with parchment paper. Bake in the oven for 20-25 minutes or until the meatballs are cooked and browned. Remove from the oven and let rest for a few minutes before serving. Serve hot.

Servings-2, Total cooking time - 30 mins
Kcal- 450, Proteins- 30g, Fats- 35g, Carbs- 1g

Beef Chuck Roast

Ingredients

- 3-4 pounds beef chuck roast
- 2 tablespoons butter or tallow
- Salt and pepper to taste
- Optional: 2 teaspoons garlic powder, 2 teaspoons onion powder, 1 teaspoon dried thyme or rosemary

Instructions

Preheat the oven to 300°F (150°C). Season the beef chuck roast with salt, pepper, garlic powder, onion powder, and thyme or rosemary. Heat butter or tallow in a Dutch oven, sear the roast on all sides, then set it aside. Add water or beef broth to cover the roast halfway, bring to a simmer, cover, and transfer to the oven. Braise for 3-4 hours until tender, then let rest for 15 minutes before slicing or shredding. Serve hot.

Servings-6, Total cooking time - 4 hrs 15 mins
Kcal- 500, Proteins- 40g, Fats- 35g, Carbs- 1g

Venison Tenderloin

Ingredients

- 1 pound venison tenderloin
- 2 tablespoons butter or tallow
- Salt and pepper to taste
- Optional: 1 teaspoon garlic powder, 1 teaspoon onion powder, 1 teaspoon dried rosemary or thyme

Instructions

Season the venison tenderloin generously with salt, pepper, garlic powder, onion powder, and dried rosemary or thyme—heat butter or tallow in a large skillet over medium-high heat. Add the venison tenderloin and sear on all sides until browned, about 2-3 minutes per side. Reduce the heat to medium and continue cooking until the internal temperature reaches 130°F (54°C) for medium-rare, about 6-8 minutes. Remove the tenderloin from the skillet and let it rest for 5-10 minutes before slicing. Serve hot.

Servings-2, Total cooking time - 20 mins
Kcal- 250, Proteins- 35g, Fats- 10g, Carbs- 2g

Bacon-Wrapped Spam Bites

Ingredients

- 1 can Spam, cut into bite-sized cubes
- 8 slices of bacon, cut in half
- Toothpicks
- Optional: 1 teaspoon garlic powder, 1 teaspoon onion powder, 1 teaspoon smoked paprika

Instructions

Preheat your oven to 400°F (200°C). Season the Spam cubes with garlic powder, onion powder, and smoked paprika if using. Wrap each Spam cube with a half slice of bacon and secure it with a toothpick. Place the bacon-wrapped Spam bites on a baking sheet lined with parchment paper. Bake in the preheated oven for 20-25 minutes or until the bacon is crispy. Remove from the oven and let rest for a few minutes before serving. Serve hot.

Servings-4, Total cooking time - 30 mins
Kcal- 350, Proteins- 15g, Fats- 30g, Carbs- 1g

Bacon-Wrapped Steak

Ingredients

- 4 small steaks (filet mignon or sirloin)
- 8 slices of bacon
- Salt and pepper to taste
- Optional: 1 teaspoon garlic powder, 1 teaspoon onion powder

Instructions

Preheat your oven to 400°F (200°C). Season the steaks with salt, pepper, garlic powder, and onion powder if using. Wrap each steak with two slices of bacon, securing with toothpicks if necessary. Heat a skillet over medium-high heat and sear the bacon-wrapped steaks on each side for 2-3 minutes until browned. Transfer the seared steaks to a baking sheet lined with parchment paper. Bake in the oven for 10-15 minutes or until the desired doneness is reached (145°F (63°C) for medium-rare). Remove from the oven and let rest for a few minutes before serving. Serve hot.

Servings-4, Total cooking time - 25 mins
Kcal- 500, Proteins- 35g, Fats- 40g, Carbs- 1g

Roast Leg of Lamb

Ingredients

- 1 leg of lamb (4-5 pounds)
- 3 tablespoons butter or tallow
- Salt and pepper to taste
- Optional: 2 teaspoons garlic powder, 2 teaspoons onion powder, 2 teaspoons dried rosemary or thyme

Instructions

Preheat your oven to 350°F (175°C). Season the leg of lamb generously with salt, pepper, garlic powder, onion powder, and dried rosemary or thyme if using. Rub the seasoning into the meat and coat with butter or tallow. Place the lamb on a roasting rack in a large roasting pan. Roast in the preheated oven for 1.5-2 hours, or until the internal temperature reaches 135°F (57°C) for medium-rare, basting occasionally with the pan juices. Remove from the oven and let the lamb rest for 15 minutes before carving. Serve hot.

Servings-7, Total cooking time - 2 hrs 15 mins
Kcal- 350, Proteins- 30g, Fats- 25g, Carbs- 1g

Lamb Kabobs

Ingredients

- 1 pound lamb leg or shoulder, cut into 1-inch cubes
- 2 tablespoons butter or tallow
- Salt and pepper to taste
- Optional: 2 teaspoons garlic powder, 2 teaspoons onion powder, 1 teaspoon dried rosemary, thyme, or oregano

Instructions

Combine the lamb cubes with butter, salt, pepper, garlic powder, onion powder, and dried herbs if using in a bowl. Mix well to coat the lamb evenly. Thread the seasoned lamb cubes onto skewers. Preheat a grill or grill pan over medium-high heat. Grill the lamb kabobs for 10-12 minutes, turning occasionally, until the lamb is cooked to your desired level of doneness. Remove from the grill and let rest for a few minutes before serving. Serve hot.

Servings-2, Total cooking time - 20 mins
Kcal- 300, Proteins- 25g, Fats- 20g, Carbs- 1g

Roasted Lamb Racks

Ingredients

- 1 rack of lamb (about 1.5 pounds)
- 2 tablespoons butter or tallow
- Salt and pepper to taste
- Optional: 1 teaspoon garlic powder, 1 teaspoon onion powder, 1 teaspoon dried rosemary or thyme

Instructions

Preheat oven to 375°F (190°C). Season the rack of lamb with salt, pepper, garlic, onion powder, and rosemary or thyme. Sear in butter or tallow for 2-3 minutes per side. Roast in the oven for 15-20 minutes until the internal temperature reaches 130°F (54°C). Let rest for 10 minutes before slicing. Serve hot.

Servings-2, Total cooking time - 35 mins
Kcal- 450, Proteins- 25g, Fats- 35g, Carbs- 1g

Bison Chuck Roast

Ingredients

- 3-4 pounds bison chuck roast
- 2 tablespoons butter or tallow
- Salt and pepper to taste
- Optional: 2 teaspoons garlic powder, 2 teaspoons onion powder, 1 teaspoon dried thyme or rosemary

Instructions

Preheat the oven to 300°F (150°C). Season the bison chuck roast with salt, pepper, garlic, onion powder, and thyme or rosemary. Sear in butter or tallow for 4-5 minutes per side. Add water or broth to cover halfway, simmer, cover, and braise in the oven for 3-4 hours until tender. Rest 15 minutes before slicing or shredding. Serve hot.

Servings-6, Total cooking time - 4 hrs 15 mins
Kcal- 400, Proteins- 50g, Fats- 20g, Carbs- 1g

<table>
<tr><td>Beef Ribs</td><td>Pork Loin Roast</td></tr>
</table>

Ingredients

- 2 racks of beef ribs (4-5 pounds)
- 2 tablespoons melted butter
- Salt and pepper to taste
- Optional: 2 teaspoons garlic powder, 2 teaspoons onion powder, 1 teaspoon smoked paprika

Ingredients

- 1 (3-4 pounds) pork loin roast
- 2 tablespoons melted butter
- 2 teaspoons sea salt
- 1 teaspoon black pepper
- Optional: 2 teaspoons garlic powder, 2 teaspoons onion powder, 1 teaspoon dried rosemary, 1 teaspoon dried thyme

Instructions

Preheat oven to 275°F (135°C). Pat beef ribs dry, rub with butter, and season with salt, pepper, garlic, onion powder, and smoked paprika. Place on a foil-lined baking sheet, cover tightly with foil, and roast for 3.5-4 hours until tender. Uncover, increase heat to 400°F (200°C), and roast for 10-15 minutes until crispy. Let rest before serving.

Servings-4, Total cooking time - 4 hrs 30 mins
Kcal- 600, Proteins- 40g, Fats- 45g, Carbs- 2g

Instructions

Preheat oven to 375°F (190°C). Pat pork loin roast dry, rub with butter, and season with salt, pepper, garlic, onion powder, rosemary, and thyme. Place on a rack in a roasting pan and roast for 1.5-2 hours, basting occasionally, until internal temperature reaches 145°F (63°C). Let rest for 10-15 minutes before slicing. Serve hot.

Servings-6, Total cooking time - 2 hrs 15 mins
Kcal- 300, Proteins- 35g, Fats- 15g, Carbs- 1g

Beef Sausages

Ingredients

- 1 pound ground beef
- 1 teaspoon salt
- 1/2 teaspoon black pepper
- Optional:1 teaspoon garlic powder, 1 teaspoon onion powder, 1 teaspoon dried thyme, 1 teaspoon smoked paprika , Sausage casings

Instructions

In a large bowl, combine the ground beef, salt, black pepper, garlic powder, onion powder, dried thyme, and smoked paprika if using. Mix until well combined. If using sausage casings, stuff the mixture into the casings according to the casing package instructions. If not using casings, shape the mixture into sausage links by hand. Heat a skillet over medium heat and cook the beef sausages for 4-5 minutes per side or until fully cooked and browned. If using casings, you can also grill or bake the sausages.

Servings-4, Total cooking time - 30 mins
Kcal- 220, Proteins- 20g, Fats- 15g, Carbs- 1g

Pork Patties

Ingredients

- 1 pound ground pork
- 1 teaspoon salt
- 1/2 teaspoon black pepper
- Butter
- Optional: 1 teaspoon onion powder, 1 teaspoon dried sage, 1/2 teaspoon dried thyme, 1/2 teaspoon crushed red pepper flakes, 1 teaspoon garlic powder

Instructions

In a large bowl, combine the ground pork, salt, black pepper, garlic powder, onion powder, dried sage, dried thyme, and crushed red pepper flakes if using. Mix until well combined. Form the mixture into patties. Heat butter in a skillet over medium heat. Cook the pork patties for about 4-5 minutes per side or until fully cooked through and browned. Serve hot.

Servings-4, Total cooking time - 15 mins
Kcal- 200, Proteins- 15g, Fats- 15g, Carbs- 1g

Homemade Pork Rinds

Ingredients

- 1 pound pork skin
- Salt to taste

Instructions

Preheat your oven to 250°F (120°C). Rinse the pork skin under cold water and pat it dry . Cut the pork skin into small, bite-sized pieces using a sharp knife. Place the pieces on a baking sheet lined with parchment paper, ensuring they are spread out in a single layer. Bake in the preheated oven for 2-3 hours until the skin is completely dried out and crispy. Remove from the oven and let it cool slightly. Increase the oven temperature to 400°F (200°C). Return the dried pork skin to the oven and bake for 5-10 minutes. Remove from the oven, sprinkle with salt, and let cool completely. Serve as a snack or use as a crunchy topping.

Servings-4, Total cooking time - 3 hrs 15 mins
Kcal- 150, Proteins- 15g, Fats- 10g, Carbs- 0g

Bacon-Wrapped Pork Chops

Ingredients

- 4 pork chops (about 1 inch thick)
- 8 slices of bacon
- Salt and pepper to taste
- Optional: 1 teaspoon garlic powder, 1 teaspoon onion powder, 1 teaspoon smoked paprika

Instructions

Preheat your oven to 400°F (200°C). Season the pork chops with salt, pepper, garlic powder, onion powder, and smoked paprika if using. Wrap each pork chop with two slices of bacon, securing with toothpicks if necessary. Place the bacon-wrapped pork chops on a baking sheet lined with parchment paper. Bake in the preheated oven for 25-30 minutes, or until the bacon is crispy and the pork chops are cooked, with an internal temperature of 145°F (63°C). Remove from the oven and let rest for a few minutes before serving. Serve hot.

Servings-4, Total cooking time - 35 mins
Kcal- 400, Proteins- 30g, Fats- 30g, Carbs- 1g

Carnivore Pizza

Ingredients

For the crust:
- 1 pound chicken or ground pork
- 1/2 cup grated raw cheese
- 1 large egg
- 1 teaspoon salt
- 1 teaspoon garlic powder (optional)

For the toppings:
- 1 cup shredded raw cheese
- 1/2 cup cooked bacon, chopped
- 1/2 cup cooked sausage, crumbled
- 1/2 cup pepperoni slices

Instructions

Preheat oven to 400°F (200°C). Mix ground meat, grated raw cheese, egg, salt, and garlic powder. Spread on a parchment-lined sheet and bake for 15-20 minutes until golden. Top with shredded cheese, bacon, sausage, and pepperoni. Bake for 10-15 minutes until cheese melts. Cool, slice, and serve hot.

Servings-4, Total cooking time - 35 mins
Kcal- 450, Proteins- 40g, Fats- 30g, Carbs- 2g

Classic Organ Meat Pie

Ingredients

- 1/3 pound beef liver, chopped
- 1/6 pound beef heart, chopped
- 1/6 pound beef kidneys, chopped
- 1/3 pound ground beef
- 1/6 cup pork rinds (fine powder)
- 1 large egg, beaten
- 1/6 cup beef broth
- 1/3 teaspoon salt
- 1/3 teaspoon black pepper
- Optional: 1/3 teaspoon garlic powder, 1/3 teaspoon onion powder

Instructions

Preheat oven to 375°F (190°C). Mix chopped liver, heart, kidneys, ground beef, pork rinds, egg, broth, salt, pepper, garlic, and onion powder. Press into a greased pie dish and bake for 45-50 minutes until cooked and browned. Let rest for 10 minutes before slicing. Serve hot.

Servings-2, Total cooking time - 1 hr 10 mins
Kcal- 400, Proteins- 40g, Fats- 25g, Carbs- 1g

Bacon-Wrapped Pork Tenderloin

Ingredients

- 1 pork tenderloin (about 1.5 pounds)
- 8-10 slices of bacon
- Salt and pepper to taste
- Optional: 1 teaspoon garlic powder, 1 teaspoon onion powder, 1 teaspoon dried thyme or rosemary

Instructions

Preheat your oven to 400°F (200°C). Season the pork tenderloin with salt, pepper, garlic powder, onion powder, and dried thyme or rosemary if using. Wrap the tenderloin with bacon slices, securing with toothpicks if necessary. Place the bacon-wrapped pork tenderloin on a baking sheet lined with parchment paper. Bake in the preheated oven for 25-30 minutes, or until the bacon is crispy and the pork tenderloin is cooked, with an internal temperature of 145°F (63°C). Remove from the oven and let rest for a few minutes before slicing. Serve hot.

Servings-4, Total cooking time - 35 mins
Kcal- 350, Proteins- 30g, Fats- 25g, Carbs- 1g

Pork Sausages

Ingredients

- 1 pound ground pork
- 1 teaspoon salt
- 1/2 teaspoon black pepper
- Optional:1 teaspoon garlic powder, 1 teaspoon onion powder, 1 teaspoon dried sage, 1/2 teaspoon dried thyme, 1/2 teaspoon crushed red pepper flakes, Sausage casings

Instructions

Mix ground pork, salt, pepper, garlic powder, onion powder, sage, thyme, and red pepper flakes. Stuff into casings or shape into links by hand. Cook in a skillet over medium heat for 4-5 minutes per side until fully cooked and browned, or grill/bake if using casings.

Servings-4, Total cooking time - 30 mins
Kcal- 200, Proteins- 15g, Fats- 15g, Carbs- 1g

Grilled Salmon Fillets

Ingredients

- 2 salmon fillets (about 6 ounces each)
- 2 tablespoons melted butter
- Salt and pepper to taste
- Optional: 1 teaspoon garlic powder, 1 teaspoon onion powder, 1 teaspoon dried dill or thyme

Instructions

Preheat your grill to medium-high heat. Season the salmon fillets with salt, pepper, garlic powder, onion powder, and dried dill or thyme. Brush the fillets with melted butter. Place the salmon fillets on the grill, skin-side down if they have skin. Grill for 4-5 minutes on each side until the salmon is opaque and flakes easily with a fork. Remove from the grill and rest for a couple of minutes before serving. Serve hot.

Servings-2, Total cooking time - 15 mins
Kcal- 300, Proteins- 25g, Fats- 20g, Carbs- 1g

Pan-Seared Tuna Steaks

Ingredients

- 2 tuna steaks (about 6 ounces each)
- 2 tablespoons butter
- Salt and pepper to taste
- Optional: 1 teaspoon garlic powder, 1 teaspoon onion powder, 1 teaspoon dried thyme or rosemary

Instructions

Season the tuna steaks with salt, pepper, garlic powder, onion powder, and dried thyme or rosemary if using. Heat butter in a skillet over medium-high heat until hot. Add the tuna steaks to the skillet. Sear the steaks for 2-3 minutes on each side for medium-rare, or adjust the time according to your preferred level of doneness. Remove from the skillet and let rest for a couple of minutes before serving. Serve hot.

Servings-2, Total cooking time - 10 mins
Kcal- 200, Proteins- 25g, Fats- 10g, Carbs- 1g

Baked Cod with Lemon Butter

Ingredients

- 2 cod fillets (about 6 ounces each)
- 2 tablespoons butter, melted
- Juice of 1 lemon
- Salt and pepper to taste
- Optional: 1 teaspoon garlic powder, 1 teaspoon onion powder, lemon slices for garnish

Instructions

Preheat your oven to 400°F (200°C). Season the cod fillets with salt, pepper, garlic powder, and onion powder if using. Place the fillets in a baking dish. In a small bowl, mix the melted butter and lemon juice. Pour the lemon butter over the cod fillets. Bake in the oven for 12-15 minutes or until the fish is opaque and flakes easily with a fork. Garnish with lemon slices if desired. Serve hot.

Servings-2, Total cooking time - 20 mins
Kcal- 200, Proteins- 20g, Fats- 12g, Carbs- 1g

Shrimp Scampi

Ingredients

- 1 pound large shrimp, peeled
- 3 tablespoons butter
- 1 teaspoon garlic powder
- Juice of 1 lemon
- Salt and pepper to taste
- Optional: 1/4 teaspoon red pepper flakes, 1 tablespoon chopped fresh parsley

Instructions

In a large skillet, melt the butter over medium heat. Add the garlic powder and cook for about 1 minute until fragrant. Add the shrimp to the skillet and season with salt, pepper, and red pepper flakes if using. Cook the shrimp on each side for 2-3 minutes until pink and opaque. Add the lemon juice to the skillet and stir to combine. Cook for 1-2 minutes until the sauce is slightly reduced. Remove from heat and garnish with fresh parsley if desired. Serve hot.

Servings-2, Total cooking time - 15 mins
Kcal- 250, Proteins- 24g, Fats- 15g, Carbs- 1g

Ingredients

- 2 lobster tails (about 6-8 ounces each)
- 4 tablespoons butter, melted
- Salt and pepper to taste
- Optional: Paprika and fresh parsley for garnish, Juice of 1 lemon, 1 teaspoon garlic powder

Instructions

Preheat your broiler on high. Using kitchen scissors, cut the top shell of each lobster tail down the center to the base and gently pull the meat out, laying it on top of the shell. Mix the melted butter, garlic powder, lemon juice, salt, and pepper in a small bowl. Brush the lobster meat generously with the butter mixture. Place the lobster tails on a baking sheet. Broil for 8-10 minutes or until the lobster meat is opaque and slightly browned on top. If desired, sprinkle with paprika and garnish with fresh parsley. Serve hot with the remaining lemon butter.

Servings-2, Total cooking time - 20 mins
Kcal- 300, Proteins- 25g, Fats- 20g, Carbs- 1g

Ingredients

- 1 pound large sea scallops
- 3 tablespoons butter
- 1 teaspoon garlic powder
- Salt and pepper to taste
- Optional: Fresh parsley for garnish

Instructions

Pat scallops dry, season with salt and pepper. Heat butter in a skillet over medium-high, sear scallops 2-3 minutes per side until golden. Remove, reduce heat, add more butter, and stir in garlic powder for 1 minute. Toss scallops in garlic butter, garnish with parsley if desired, and serve hot.

Servings-2, Total cooking time - 10 mins
Kcal- 300, Proteins- 25g, Fats- 20g, Carbs- 1g

Ingredients

- 2 catfish fillets (about 6 ounces each)
- 2 tablespoons melted butter or tallow
- 1 teaspoon salt
- 1 teaspoon black pepper
- Optional:1 teaspoon garlic powder, 1 teaspoon onion powder, 1 teaspoon smoked paprika, 1/2 teaspoon cayenne pepper

Instructions

Preheat a cast-iron skillet over high heat until it is smoking hot. While the skillet is heating, brush both sides of the catfish fillets with melted butter or tallow. In a small bowl, mix the salt, black pepper, garlic powder, onion powder, smoked paprika, and cayenne pepper if used. Generously coat both sides of the fillets with the spice mixture. Place the fillets in the hot skillet and cook on each side for 3-4 minutes until the fish is blackened and cooked through. Serve hot.

Servings-2, Total cooking time - 15 mins
Kcal- 300, Proteins- 25g, Fats- 20g, Carbs- 1g

Ingredients

- 2 pounds crab legs (king or snow crab)
- 1 cup water
- 1/2 cup butter, melted

Instructions

In a large pot, bring 1 cup of water to a boil. Place a steamer basket in the pot and arrange the crab legs in the basket. Cover and steam for 5-7 minutes or until the crab legs are heated. While the crab legs are steaming, melt the butter in a small saucepan over low heat. Once the crab legs are done, remove them from the pot and transfer them to a serving platter. If desired, serve the steamed crab legs hot with the drawn butter.

Servings-2, Total cooking time - 15 mins
Kcal- 450, Proteins- 40g, Fats- 30g, Carbs- 1g

Garlic Butter Clams

Ingredients

- 2 pounds fresh clams
- 4 tablespoons butter
- 1/2 teaspoon salt
- 1/4 teaspoon black pepper
- Optional: 1/4 teaspoon red pepper flakes, 1 teaspoon garlic powder fresh parsley for garnish

Instructions

In a large pot, melt the butter over medium heat. Add the garlic powder, salt, black pepper, and red pepper flakes if using. Stir to combine. Add the clams to the pot and pour in 1/2 cup of water. Cover the pot with a lid and steam the clams for 5-7 minutes or until all the clams have opened. Discard any clams that do not open. Remove from heat and transfer the clams to a serving bowl. Pour the garlic butter sauce over the clams. Garnish with fresh parsley if desired, and serve hot.

Servings-2, Total cooking time - 15 mins
Kcal- 350, Proteins- 25g, Fats- 25g, Carbs- 6g

Fried Calamari Rings

Ingredients

- 1 pound calamari rings
- 2 large eggs
- 1 cup pork rinds, crushed
- Salt and pepper to taste
- Tallow or lard for frying
- Optional : 1 teaspoon garlic powder, 1 teaspoon onion powder

Instructions

Heat tallow or lard in a deep skillet or pot over medium-high heat until it reaches 350°F (175°C). In a bowl, whisk the eggs with a pinch of salt and pepper. Place the crushed pork rinds in another bowl. Season the calamari rings with salt, pepper, garlic powder, and onion powder if using. Dip each calamari ring into the beaten eggs, then coat with the crushed pork rinds. Fry the coated calamari rings in the hot oil for 2-3 minutes, or until golden brown and crispy. Remove from the oil and drain on paper towels.

Servings-2, Total cooking time - 20 mins
Kcal- 400, Proteins- 30g, Fats- 30g, Carbs- 2g

Grilled Octopus Tentacles

Ingredients

- 2-3 octopus tentacles (about 1.5 pounds)
- 3 tablespoons butter or tallow
- Salt and pepper to taste
- Optional: 1 teaspoon garlic powder, 1 teaspoon smoked paprika

Instructions

In a large pot, bring water to a boil. Add the octopus tentacles and simmer for 45-60 minutes until tender. Remove the tentacles from the pot and let them cool slightly. Preheat your grill to medium-high heat. Brush the tentacles with butter or tallow and season with salt, pepper, garlic powder, and smoked paprika if using. Grill the tentacles on each side for 4-5 minutes until they are charred and crispy. Remove from the grill and let rest for a few minutes.

Servings-2, Total cooking time - 1 hr 30 mins
Kcal- 300, Proteins- 25g, Fats- 20g, Carbs- 2g

Bacon-Wrapped Pan-Seared Scallops

Ingredients

- 1 pound large sea scallops
- 8 slices bacon (about 1 slice per scallop)
- Salt and pepper to taste
- 1 teaspoon garlic powder
- 1 tablespoon butter

Instructions

Pat the scallops dry with paper towels and season with salt, pepper, and garlic powder. Wrap each scallop with a slice of bacon and secure with a toothpick—heat butter in a large skillet over medium-high heat. Add the bacon-wrapped scallops to the skillet, ensuring not to overcrowd the pan. Sear the scallops on each side for 3-4 minutes until the bacon is crispy and the scallops are cooked through. Remove from the skillet and let rest for a few minutes.

Servings-2, Total cooking time - 20 mins
Kcal- 450, Proteins- 30g, Fats- 35g, Carbs- 2g

Grilled Sardines

Ingredients

- 1 pound fresh sardines, cleaned and gutted
- 2 tablespoons butter
- Salt and pepper to taste
- Optional: 1 teaspoon garlic powder, 1 teaspoon smoked paprika

Instructions

Preheat your grill to medium-high heat. Rinse the sardines under cold water and pat dry with paper towels. Brush the sardines with butter and season with salt, pepper, garlic powder, and smoked paprika if using. Place the sardines on the grill and cook for 3-4 minutes on each side until the skin is crispy and the fish is cooked through. Remove from the grill and let rest for a few minutes.

Servings-2, Total cooking time - 15 mins
Kcal- 250, Proteins- 25g, Fats- 15g, Carbs- 1g

Carnivore Crab Cakes

Ingredients

- 1 pound lump crab meat
- 1/2 cup crushed pork rinds
- 2 large eggs, beaten
- Salt and pepper to taste
- 2 tablespoons tallow or lard for frying
- Optional : 1 teaspoon garlic powder, 1 teaspoon onion powder

Instructions

In a large bowl, combine the crab meat, crushed pork rinds, beaten eggs, garlic powder, onion powder, dried dill (if using), salt, and pepper. Mix gently until well combined. Form the mixture into 6-8 patties. Heat tallow or lard in a large skillet over medium-high heat. Fry the crab cakes on each side for 3-4 minutes until golden brown and crispy. Remove from the skillet and drain on paper towels. Serve hot.

Servings-2, Total cooking time - 20 mins
Kcal- 350, Proteins- 30g, Fats- 25g, Carbs- 1g

Grilled Shrimp and Scallop Skewers

Ingredients

- 1/2 pound large shrimp
- 1/2 pound large sea scallops
- 3 tablespoons melted butter
- Salt and pepper to taste
- Optional: 1 teaspoon garlic powder, 1 teaspoon onion powder, 1 teaspoon smoked paprika

Instructions

Preheat your grill to medium-high heat. In a bowl, combine melted butter with salt, pepper, garlic powder, onion powder, and smoked paprika if using. Thread the shrimp and scallops onto skewers, alternating between the two. Brush the seafood with the butter mixture. Place the skewers on the grill and cook for 2-3 minutes on each side until the shrimp are pink and opaque and the scallops are firm and cooked through. Remove from the grill and let rest for a few minutes.

Servings-2, Total cooking time - 20 mins
Kcal- 300, Proteins- 25g, Fats- 20g, Carbs- 2g

Lemon Pepper Grilled Salmon

Ingredients

- 2 salmon fillets (about 6 ounces each)
- 2 tablespoons melted butter
- 1 tablespoon lemon zest
- 1 tablespoon freshly ground black pepper
- 1 teaspoon salt
- Juice of 1 lemon

Instructions

Preheat your grill to medium-high heat. In a small bowl, mix the melted butter, lemon zest, black pepper, and salt. Brush the salmon fillets with the mixture on both sides. Place the salmon fillets on the grill, skin-side down if they have skin. Grill 4-5 minutes on each side, or until the salmon is opaque and flakes easily with a fork. Remove from the grill and squeeze fresh lemon juice over the top. Serve hot.

Servings-2, Total cooking time - 15 mins
Kcal- 300, Proteins- 25g, Fats- 20g, Carbs- 1g

Bacon Wrapped Cod

Ingredients

- 2 cod fillets (about 6 ounces each)
- 4 slices of bacon
- Salt and pepper to taste
- Optional: 1 teaspoon garlic powder, 1 teaspoon onion powder

Instructions

Preheat your oven to 400°F (200°C). Season the cod fillets with salt, pepper, garlic powder, and onion powder if using. Wrap each cod fillet with two slices of bacon, securing with toothpicks if necessary. Place the bacon-wrapped cod fillets on a baking sheet lined with parchment paper. Bake in the preheated oven for 15-20 minutes, or until the bacon is crispy and the cod is cooked and flakes easily with a fork. Remove the toothpicks before serving. Serve hot.

Servings-2, Total cooking time - 25 mins
Kcal- 350, Proteins- 35g, Fats- 20g, Carbs- 1g

Garlic Butter Grilled Prawns

Ingredients

- 1 pound large prawns, peeled and deveined
- 3 tablespoons butter, melted
- 1 teaspoon garlic powder
- 1 teaspoon lemon juice
- Salt and pepper to taste
- Optional: Fresh parsley for garnish

Instructions

Preheat your grill to medium-high heat. In a small bowl, mix the melted butter, garlic powder, lemon juice, salt, and pepper. Brush the prawns with the garlic butter mixture on both sides. Place the prawns on the grill and cook for 2-3 minutes on each side until they are pink and opaque. Remove from the grill and brush with any remaining garlic butter. Garnish with fresh parsley, if desired. Serve hot.

Servings-2, Total cooking time - 15 mins
Kcal- 250, Proteins- 24g, Fats- 15g, Carbs- 1g

Bacon Wrapped Shrimp

Ingredients

- 1 pound large shrimp, peeled and deveined, tails on
- 12 slices of bacon, cut in half
- Salt and pepper to taste
- Optional: Lemon wedges for serving, 1 teaspoon garlic powder, 1 teaspoon onion powder

Instructions

Preheat your oven to 400°F (200°C). Season the shrimp with garlic, onion, salt, and pepper. Wrap each shrimp with a half slice of bacon, securing it with a toothpick if necessary. Place the bacon-wrapped shrimp on a baking sheet lined with parchment paper. Bake in the oven for 12-15 minutes or until the bacon is crispy and the shrimp are cooked. Optionally, serve with lemon wedges. Serve hot.

Servings-4, Total cooking time - 20 mins
Kcal- 250, Proteins- 20g, Fats- 18g, Carbs- 1g

Smoked Salmon Deviled Eggs

Ingredients

- 6 large eggs
- 3 ounces smoked salmon, chopped
- 3 tablespoons mayonnaise (made from animal fat)
- 1 teaspoon Dijon mustard
- 1/2 teaspoon garlic powder
- Salt and pepper to taste
- Optional: Fresh parsley for garnish

Instructions

Boil eggs for 10 minutes, cool in an ice bath, then peel and halve—mash yolks with mayonnaise, Dijon mustard, garlic powder, salt, and pepper. Fill egg whites with the mixture, fold in smoked salmon, and garnish with parsley if desired. Serve chilled.

Servings-6, Total cooking time - 20 mins
Kcal- 120, Proteins- 7g, Fats- 10g, Carbs- 1g

Grilled Chicken Thighs

Ingredients

- 4 bone-in, skin-on chicken thighs
- 2 tablespoons melted butter
- Salt and pepper to taste
- Optional: 1 teaspoon garlic powder, 1 teaspoon onion powder, 1 teaspoon paprika

Instructions

Preheat your grill to medium-high heat. Pat the chicken thighs dry with paper towels. Brush the chicken thighs with melted butter on both sides. Season generously with salt, pepper, garlic powder, onion powder, and paprika if using. Place the chicken thighs on the grill, skin-side down. Grill for 5-7 minutes per side until the internal temperature reaches 165°F (74°C) and the skin is crispy and golden brown.

Servings-2, Total cooking time - 25 mins
Kcal- 400, Proteins- 25g, Fats- 30g, Carbs- 1g

Roast Chicken with Herb Butter

Ingredients

- 1 whole chicken (about 4-5 pounds)
- 1/2 cup butter, softened
- 2 teaspoons garlic powder
- 2 teaspoons onion powder
- 1 teaspoon dried thyme
- 1 teaspoon dried rosemary
- 1 teaspoon dried sage
- Salt and pepper to taste

Instructions

Preheat your oven to 375°F (190°C). Mix the butter with garlic powder, onion powder, thyme, rosemary, sage, salt, and pepper. Loosen the skin of the chicken and spread half the herb butter under it. Rub the remaining butter over the outside. Place the chicken on a roasting rack in a pan. Roast for 1.5-2 hours, until the internal temperature reaches 165°F (74°C) and the skin is golden brown.

Servings-5, Total cooking time - 2 hrs 15 mins
Kcal- 500, Proteins- 30g, Fats- 35g, Carbs- 1g

Chicken Wings

Ingredients

- 2 pounds chicken wings
- 2 tablespoons melted butter
- Salt and pepper to taste
- Optional: 1 teaspoon garlic powder, 1 teaspoon onion powder, 1 teaspoon paprika

Instructions

Preheat your oven to 400°F (200°C). Pat the chicken wings dry with paper towels. Toss the wings in melted butter, then season with salt, pepper, garlic powder, onion powder, and paprika if using. Arrange the wings in a single layer on a baking sheet lined with parchment paper. Bake in the oven for 40-45 minutes, turning halfway through, until the wings are crispy and golden brown. Serve hot.

Servings-4, Total cooking time - 50 mins
Kcal- 300, Proteins- 25g, Fats- 20g, Carbs- 2g

Pan-Seared Duck Breast

Ingredients

- 2 duck breasts
- Salt and pepper to taste
- Optional: 1 teaspoon garlic powder, 1 teaspoon onion powder, 1 teaspoon dried thyme

Instructions

Score the skin of the duck breasts in a crosshatch pattern, being careful not to cut into the meat. Season both sides of the duck breasts with salt, pepper, garlic powder, onion powder, and dried thyme if using. Place the duck breasts skin-side down in a cold skillet. Turn the heat to medium and cook for 6-8 minutes until the skin is crispy and golden brown. Flip the duck breasts and cook for 3-4 minutes for medium-rare, or adjust the time according to your preferred level of doneness. Remove from the skillet and let rest for 5 minutes before slicing. Serve hot.

Servings-2, Total cooking time - 20 mins
Kcal- 400, Proteins- 25g, Fats- 30g, Carbs- 1g

Roasted Turkey Drumsticks

Ingredients

- 2 turkey drumsticks
- 2 tablespoons melted butter
- Salt and pepper to taste
- Optional: 1 teaspoon garlic powder, 1 teaspoon onion powder, 1 teaspoon dried thyme or rosemary

Instructions

Preheat your oven to 375°F (190°C). Pat the turkey drumsticks dry with paper towels. Brush the drumsticks with melted butter, then season with salt, pepper, garlic powder, onion powder, and dried thyme or rosemary if using. Place the drumsticks on a baking sheet lined with parchment paper or in a roasting pan. Roast in the oven for 1.5-2 hours until the internal temperature reaches 165°F (74°C) and the skin is golden brown and crispy. Let rest for 10 minutes before serving. Serve hot.

Servings-2, Total cooking time - 2 hours
Kcal- 450, Proteins- 40g, Fats- 30g, Carbs- 2g

Chicken Burger Patties

Ingredients

- 1 pound ground chicken
- 1/2 cup pork rinds, crushed into a fine powder
- 1 large egg
- 1 teaspoon salt
- 1/2 teaspoon black pepper
- Optional: 1 teaspoon garlic powder, 1 teaspoon onion powder

Instructions

Combine the ground chicken, crushed pork rinds, egg, salt, pepper, garlic powder, and onion powder in a large bowl. Mix until well combined. Form the mixture into 4 equal patties. Heat a skillet over medium heat. Cook the chicken patties for about 5-6 minutes per side or until fully cooked through and browned. Serve hot.

Servings-4, Total cooking time - 20 mins
Kcal- 200, Proteins- 25g, Fats- 10g, Carbs- 1g

Duck Confit

Ingredients

- 4 duck legs
- 1/4 cup salt
- Duck fat (enough to submerge the legs, about 2-3 cups)
- Optional: 1 teaspoon garlic powder, 2 teaspoons dried thyme, 2 teaspoons black pepper

Instructions

Rub duck legs with salt, garlic powder, thyme, and pepper. Refrigerate for 24 hours. Preheat oven to 225°F (110°C), rinse, and pat the legs dry. Cover with duck fat in an oven-safe pot, and cook for 2.5-3 hours until tender. Drain, then sear skin-side down in a skillet for crispy skin. Serve hot.

**Servings-4, Total cooking time - 3 hrs 15 mins
Kcal- 700, Proteins- 30g, Fats- 60g, Carbs- 2g**

Grilled Chicken Breast

Ingredients

- 2 boneless, skinless chicken breasts
- 2 tablespoons butter
- Salt and pepper to taste
- Optional: 1 teaspoon garlic powder, 1 teaspoon onion powder, 1 teaspoon dried thyme or rosemary

Instructions

Preheat your grill to medium-high heat. Pat the chicken breasts dry with paper towels. Brush the chicken breasts with butter and season with salt, pepper, garlic powder, onion powder, and dried thyme or rosemary if using. Place the chicken breasts on the grill and cook for 6-8 minutes on each side, or until the internal temperature reaches 165°F (74°C). Remove from the grill and let rest for 5 minutes before serving. Serve hot.

**Servings-2, Total cooking time - 20 mins
Kcal- 250, Proteins- 30g, Fats- 12g, Carbs- 1g**

Chicken Hearts Skewers

Ingredients

- 1 pound chicken hearts
- 2 tablespoons melted butter
- Salt and pepper to taste
- Optional: 1 teaspoon garlic powder, 1 teaspoon smoked paprika, 1 teaspoon dried thyme

Instructions

Preheat your grill to medium-high heat. Rinse and pat the chicken hearts dry with paper towels. In a bowl, toss the chicken hearts with melted butter, salt, pepper, garlic powder, smoked paprika, and dried thyme if using. Thread the seasoned chicken hearts onto skewers. Place the skewers on the grill and cook for 4-5 minutes on each side, or until the hearts are cooked through and have a nice char. Remove from the grill and let rest for a few minutes before serving. Serve hot.

Servings-2, Total cooking time - 20 mins
Kcal- 250, Proteins- 25g, Fats- 15g, Carbs- 1g

Carnivore Turkey Burgers

Ingredients

- 1 pound ground turkey
- 1 teaspoon salt
- 1/2 teaspoon black pepper
- Optional: 1 teaspoon garlic powder, 1 teaspoon onion powder

Instructions

In a bowl, combine ground turkey with salt, pepper, garlic powder, and onion powder if using. Mix until well combined. Divide the mixture into 4 equal portions and shape each into a patty. Heat a skillet or grill over medium-high heat. Cook the patties on each side for 4-5 minutes until they reach an internal temperature of 165°F (74°C) and are no longer pink in the center. Remove from the skillet or grill and rest for a few minutes before serving. Serve hot.

Servings-2, Total cooking time - 15 mins
Kcal- 200, Proteins- 25g, Fats- 10g, Carbs- 1g

Roast Duck

Ingredients

- 1 whole duck (about 5-6 pounds)
- Salt and pepper to taste
- Optional: 1 teaspoon garlic powder, 1 teaspoon onion powder

Instructions

Preheat your oven to 375°F (190°C). Pat the duck dry with paper towels. Season the duck generously with salt, pepper, garlic powder, onion powder, and dried thyme or rosemary if using. Place the duck on a rack in a roasting pan, breast side up. Roast in the oven for 1.5-2 hours until the internal temperature reaches 165°F (74°C) and the skin is crispy and golden brown. Baste the duck with its fat occasionally during roasting. Let the duck rest for 15 minutes before carving. Serve hot.

**Servings-4, Total cooking time - 2 hrs 15 mins
Kcal- 450, Proteins- 25g, Fats- 35g, Carbs- 2g**

Smoked Turkey Legs

Ingredients

- 2 turkey legs
- 2 tablespoons melted butter
- Salt and pepper to taste
- Optional: 1 teaspoon garlic powder, 1 teaspoon onion powder, 1 teaspoon smoked paprika

Instructions

Preheat your smoker to 225°F (110°C). Pat the turkey legs dry with paper towels. Brush the turkey legs with melted butter, then season with salt, pepper, garlic powder, onion powder, and smoked paprika if using. Place the turkey legs in the smoker. Smoke for 3-4 hours or until the internal temperature reaches 165°F (74°C). Remove from the smoker and let rest for 10 minutes before serving. Serve hot.

**Servings-2, Total cooking time - 4 hrs 15 mins
Kcal- 500, Proteins- 50g, Fats- 30g, Carbs- 1g**

Roast Quail

Ingredients

- 4 whole quails
- 2 tablespoons melted butter
- Salt and pepper to taste
- Optional: 1 teaspoon garlic powder, 1 teaspoon onion powder, 1 teaspoon dried thyme or rosemary

Instructions

Preheat your oven to 400°F (200°C). Pat the quails dry with paper towels. Brush the quails with melted butter, then season with salt, pepper, garlic powder, onion powder, and dried thyme or rosemary if using. Place the quails on a roasting pan or baking sheet. Roast in the preheated oven for 20-25 minutes, or until the internal temperature reaches 165°F (74°C) and the skin is golden brown and crispy. Let the quails rest for 5 minutes before serving. Serve hot.

Servings-2, Total cooking time - 30 mins
Kcal- 350, Proteins- 30g, Fats- 25g, Carbs- 1g

Turkey Bacon Strips

Ingredients

- 1 pound turkey bacon
- Optional: 1 tablespoon butter or tallow (for extra crispiness)

Instructions

Heat a large skillet over medium-high heat. Add butter or tallow to the skillet for extra crispiness if desired. Lay the turkey bacon strips in the skillet in a single layer. Cook for 2-3 minutes on each side or until they reach your desired level of crispiness. Remove from the skillet and drain on paper towels. Serve hot.

Servings-4, Total cooking time - 10 mins
Kcal- 100, Proteins- 6g, Fats- 8g, Carbs- 1g

Ingredients

- 1 pound chicken breast or thighs, cut into 1-inch cubes
- 2 tablespoons butter
- Salt and pepper to taste
- Optional: 1 teaspoon garlic powder, 1 teaspoon onion powder, 1 teaspoon paprika

Instructions

Preheat your grill to medium-high heat. In a bowl, toss the chicken cubes with butter, salt, pepper, garlic powder, onion powder, and paprika if using. Thread the seasoned chicken onto skewers. Place the skewers on the grill and cook for 4-5 minutes on each side until the chicken is cooked and has a nice char. Remove from the grill and let rest for a few minutes. Serve hot.

Servings-2, Total cooking time - 20 mins
Kcal- 300, Proteins- 35g, Fats- 15g, Carbs- 1g

Ingredients

- 1 pound ground turkey
- 1/4 cup finely minced pork rinds
- 1 large egg, beaten
- 1 teaspoon salt
- 1/2 teaspoon black pepper
- Optional: 1 teaspoon garlic powder, 1 teaspoon onion powder

Instructions

Preheat your oven to 375°F (190°C). Combine ground turkey, minced pork rinds (if using), beaten egg, salt, pepper, garlic powder, and onion powder in a bowl. Mix until well combined. Form the mixture into 12-15 meatballs, about 1.5 inches in diameter each. Place the meatballs on a baking sheet lined with parchment paper. Bake in the oven for 20-25 minutes or until the meatballs are cooked and browned.

Servings-3, Total cooking time - 30 mins
Kcal- 250, Proteins- 25g, Fats- 15g, Carbs- 1g

Ingredients

- 1 pound ground turkey
- 1 teaspoon salt
- 1/2 teaspoon black pepper
- Optional: 1/2 teaspoon crushed red pepper flakes, 1 teaspoon garlic powder, 1 teaspoon onion powder, 1 teaspoon dried sage, 1/2 teaspoon dried thyme, Sausage casings

Instructions

In a large bowl, combine ground turkey, salt, black pepper, garlic powder, onion powder, dried sage, dried thyme, and crushed red pepper flakes if using. Mix until well combined. If using sausage casings, stuff the mixture into the casings. If not, shape it into sausage links by hand. Heat a skillet over medium heat and cook the sausages for 4-5 minutes per side or until fully cooked and browned. Alternatively, you can grill or bake the sausages.

Servings-3, Total cooking time - 30 mins
Kcal- 200, Proteins- 22g, Fats- 10g, Carbs- 1g

Ingredients

- 4 bone-in, skin-on chicken thighs
- 2 tablespoons butter
- 1 tablespoon lemon zest
- 1 teaspoon black pepper
- 1 teaspoon salt

Instructions

Preheat your oven to 375°F (190°C). Pat the chicken thighs dry with paper towels. Mix the butter, lemon zest, black pepper, and salt in a small bowl. Rub the mixture evenly over the chicken thighs. Place the thighs on a baking sheet lined with parchment paper or baking dish. Bake in the preheated oven for 35-40 minutes, or until the internal temperature reaches 165°F (74°C) and the skin is crispy and golden brown.

Servings-2, Total cooking time - 45 mins
Kcal- 400, Proteins- 25g, Fats- 30g, Carbs- 1g

Ingredients

- 1 pound turkey breast cutlets
- 2 tablespoons melted butter
- Salt and pepper to taste
- Optional: 1 teaspoon garlic powder, 1 teaspoon onion powder

Instructions

Pat the turkey breast cutlets dry with paper towels. Season with salt, pepper, garlic powder, and onion powder if using. Heat the melted butter in a large skillet over medium-high heat. Add the turkey cutlets to the skillet and cook for 3-4 minutes on each side until golden brown and cooked through. Remove from the skillet and let rest for a few minutes before serving. Serve hot.

Servings-2, Total cooking time - 15 mins
Kcal- 250, Proteins- 30g, Fats- 12g, Carbs- 1g

Ingredients

- 2 pounds chicken wings
- 1/2 cup duck fat
- Salt and pepper to taste
- Optional: 1 teaspoon garlic powder, 1 teaspoon onion powder

Instructions

Pat the chicken wings dry with paper towels. Season with salt, pepper, garlic powder, and onion powder if using. Heat the duck fat in a large skillet or deep fryer over medium-high heat until hot. Add the chicken wings in batches, carefully not to overcrowd the pan. Fry the wings for 8-10 minutes, turning occasionally until golden brown and crispy. Remove the wings from the skillet and drain on paper towels. Repeat with the remaining wings. Serve hot.

Servings-4, Total cooking time - 30 mins
Kcal- 350, Proteins- 25g, Fats- 25g, Carbs- 1g

Chicken Liver Sauté

Ingredients

- 1 pound chicken livers, trimmed and cleaned
- 3 tablespoons duck fat or butter
- Salt and pepper to taste
- Optional: 1 teaspoon garlic powder, 1 teaspoon onion powder, 1 teaspoon dried thyme

Instructions

Pat the chicken livers dry with paper towels. Season with salt, pepper, garlic powder, onion powder, and dried thyme if using. Heat the duck fat or butter in a large skillet over medium-high heat. Add the chicken livers to the skillet and cook on each side for 4-5 minutes until they are browned and cooked through but still slightly pink in the center. Remove from the skillet and let rest for a few minutes before serving. Serve hot.

**Servings-2, Total cooking time - 15 mins
Kcal- 300, Proteins- 25g, Fats- 20g, Carbs- 1g**

Roast Chicken Drumsticks

Ingredients

- 8 chicken drumsticks
- 2 tablespoons melted butter
- Salt and pepper to taste
- Optional: 1 teaspoon garlic powder, 1 teaspoon onion powder, 1 teaspoon paprika

Instructions

Preheat your oven to 400°F (200°C). Pat the chicken drumsticks dry with paper towels. Toss the drumsticks in melted butter, then season with salt, pepper, garlic powder, onion powder, and paprika if using. Arrange the drumsticks in a single layer on a baking sheet lined with parchment paper or in a roasting pan. Roast in the preheated oven for 35-40 minutes, turning halfway through, until the drumsticks are cooked and the skin is crispy and golden brown. Serve hot.

**Servings-4, Total cooking time - 45 mins
Kcal- 300, Proteins- 25g, Fats- 20g, Carbs- 1g**

Ingredients

- 1 whole goose (about 10-12 pounds)
- 1/2 cup butter, softened
- Salt and pepper to taste
- Optional: 2 teaspoons garlic powder, 2 teaspoons onion powder, 1 teaspoon dried thyme, 1 teaspoon dried rosemary, 1 teaspoon dried sage

Ingredients

- 2 pounds chicken bones (backs, necks, wings, or a whole carcass)
- 2 tablespoons apple cider vinegar
- 1 teaspoon salt
- 10 cups water
- Optional: 1 teaspoon black peppercorns, 2 bay leaves

Instructions

Preheat oven to 325°F (165°C). Pat the goose dry and rub with a mixture of butter, garlic powder, onion powder, thyme, rosemary, sage, salt, and pepper. Place on a rack in a roasting pan, breast side up, and roast for 3-4 hours until the thigh reaches 165°F (74°C). Baste occasionally. Let rest for 20 minutes before serving.

Servings-7, Total cooking time - 4 hrs 30 mins
Kcal- 700, Proteins- 40g, Fats- 60g, Carbs- 1g

Instructions

Place chicken bones in a pot, add apple cider vinegar, salt, and water, and let sit for 30 minutes. Add peppercorns and bay leaves if using. Bring to a boil, then simmer for 12-24 hours, skimming off impurities. Strain, discard solids, and cool. Store in the fridge or freeze. Serve hot.

Servings-8, Total cooking time -16 hours
Kcal- 50, Proteins- 6g, Fats- 2g, Carbs- 1g

Ingredients

- 2 pounds boneless, skinless chicken breasts or thighs
- Salt and pepper to taste
- Optional: 1 teaspoon garlic powder, 1 teaspoon onion powder, 1 teaspoon dried thyme or rosemary

Instructions

Place the chicken in a large pot and cover with water. Season with salt, pepper, garlic powder, onion powder, and dried herbs if using. Bring the water to a boil over medium-high heat, then reduce the heat to low and simmer for 20-25 minutes, or until the chicken is cooked through and easily shreds with a fork. Remove the chicken from the pot and let it cool slightly. Using two forks or your hands, shred the chicken into bite-sized pieces. Serve hot.

Servings-4, Total cooking time - 30 mins
Kcal- 200, Proteins- 36g, Fats- 4g, Carbs- 0g

Ingredients

- 2 pounds chicken wings
- 2 tablespoons melted butter
- Salt and pepper to taste
- Optional: 1 teaspoon garlic powder, 1 teaspoon onion powder, 1 teaspoon smoked paprika

Instructions

Preheat the smoker to 250°F (120°C). Pat chicken wings dry, toss in melted butter, and season with salt, pepper, garlic powder, onion powder, and smoked paprika. Smoke wings for 1.5-2 hours until they reach 165°F (74°C). For crispy skin, bake at 425°F (220°C) for 20-25 minutes. Serve hot.

Servings-4, Total cooking time -2 hrs 30 mins
Kcal- 300, Proteins- 25g, Fats- 20g, Carbs- 1g

Salt and Vinegar Wings

Ingredients

- 2 pounds chicken wings
- 2 tablespoons melted butter
- 1/4 cup apple cider vinegar
- 2 teaspoons sea salt
- Optional: 1 teaspoon garlic powder, 1 teaspoon onion powder

Instructions

Preheat your oven to 400°F (200°C). Pat the chicken wings dry with paper towels. Toss the wings in melted butter. Arrange the wings in a single layer on a baking sheet lined with parchment paper. Bake in the preheated oven for 35-40 minutes, turning halfway through, until the wings are crispy and golden brown. While the wings are baking, combine the apple cider vinegar, sea salt, garlic powder, and onion powder in a large bowl. Once the wings are done, mix them in the vinegar mixture until well coated. Serve hot.

Servings-4, Total cooking time - 45 mins
Kcal- 250, Proteins- 20g, Fats- 18g, Carbs- 1g

Carnivore Fried Chicken

Ingredients

- 2 pounds chicken pieces
- 2 cups pork rinds, crushed
- 2 large eggs
- 1/2 cup heavy cream
- 1 teaspoon salt
- 1 teaspoon black pepper
- Tallow or lard for frying
- Optional: 1 teaspoon garlic powder, 1 teaspoon onion powder, 1 teaspoon paprika

Instructions

Whisk eggs with heavy cream. Mix crushed pork rinds with salt, pepper, garlic powder, onion powder, and paprika. Dip chicken pieces in egg mixture, then coat in pork rind mixture. Heat tallow or lard in a skillet to 350°F (175°C). Fry chicken in batches for 8-10 minutes per side until golden brown and cooked. Drain on paper towels.

Servings-4, Total cooking time -45 mins
Kcal- 500, Proteins- 40g, Fats- 35g, Carbs- 2g

Bacon Wrapped Chicken Legs

Ingredients

- 6 chicken legs (drumsticks)
- 12 slices of bacon
- Salt and pepper to taste
- Optional: 1 teaspoon garlic powder, 1 teaspoon onion powder, 1 teaspoon paprika

Instructions

Preheat your oven to 400°F (200°C). Season the chicken legs with salt, pepper, garlic powder, onion powder, and paprika if using. Wrap each chicken leg with two slices of bacon, securing with toothpicks if necessary. Place the bacon-wrapped chicken legs on a baking sheet lined with parchment paper. Bake in the preheated oven for 35-40 minutes, or until the bacon is crispy and the chicken is cooked, with an internal temperature of 165°F (74°C). Remove from the oven and let rest for a few minutes before serving. Serve hot.

Servings-6, Total cooking time - 45 mins
Kcal- 350, Proteins- 28g, Fats- 25g, Carbs- 1g

Bacon-Wrapped Chicken Breasts

Ingredients

- 4 boneless, skinless chicken breasts
- 8 slices of bacon
- Salt and pepper to taste
- Optional: 1 teaspoon garlic powder, 1 teaspoon onion powder, 1 teaspoon paprika

Instructions

Preheat your oven to 400°F (200°C). Season the chicken breasts with salt, pepper, garlic powder, onion powder, and paprika if using. Wrap each chicken breast with two slices of bacon, securing with toothpicks if necessary. Place the bacon-wrapped chicken breasts on a baking sheet lined with parchment paper. Bake in the preheated oven for 25-30 minutes, or until the bacon is crispy and the chicken is cooked, with an internal temperature of 165°F (74°C). Remove from the oven and let rest for a few minutes before serving. Serve hot.

Servings-4, Total cooking time -35 mins
Kcal- 400, Proteins- 35g, Fats- 25g, Carbs- 1g

| **Chicken Meatballs** | **Chicken Skin Chips** |

Ingredients

- 1 pound ground chicken
- 1/2 cup pork rinds, crushed into a fine powder
- 1 large egg
- 1 teaspoon salt
- 1/2 teaspoon black pepper
- Optional: 1 teaspoon garlic powder, 1 teaspoon onion powder

Instructions

Preheat your oven to 375°F (190°C). Combine the ground chicken, crushed pork rinds, egg, salt, pepper, garlic powder, and onion powder in a large bowl. Mix until well combined. Form the mixture into small meatballs, about 1.5 inches in diameter. Place the meatballs on a baking sheet lined with parchment paper. Bake in the oven for 20-25 minutes or until the meatballs are cooked and browned. Serve hot.

Servings-4, Total cooking time - 30 mins
Kcal- 200, Proteins- 25g, Fats- 10g, Carbs- 1g

Ingredients

- Chicken skin (from about 2-3 pounds of chicken)
- Salt to taste
- Optional: 1 teaspoon garlic powder, 1 teaspoon onion powder, 1 teaspoon paprika

Instructions

Preheat your oven to 375°F (190°C). Lay the chicken skins flat on a baking sheet lined with parchment paper. Sprinkle with salt and optional seasonings like garlic powder, onion powder, and paprika. Bake in the oven for 30-40 minutes or until the skins are golden brown and crispy. Remove from the oven and let cool on a wire rack. Serve hot.

Servings-4, Total cooking time -45 mins
Kcal- 150, Proteins- 10g, Fats- 12g, Carbs- 1g

Bacon-Wrapped Turkey

Ingredients

- 1 whole turkey (10-12 pounds)
- 1 pound bacon slices
- Salt and pepper to taste
- Optional: 2 teaspoons garlic powder, 2 teaspoons onion powder, 1 teaspoon dried thyme, 1 teaspoon dried rosemary

Instructions

Preheat oven to 325°F (165°C). Season the turkey with salt, pepper, garlic powder, onion powder, thyme, and rosemary. Wrap the turkey in bacon, securing it with toothpicks if needed. Place on a rack in a roasting pan and roast for 3-4 hours, basting occasionally, until the thigh reaches 165°F (74°C) and the bacon is crispy. Rest for 20 minutes before carving. Serve hot.

**Servings-11, Total cooking time - 4 hr 30 mins
Kcal- 600, Proteins- 55g, Fats- 40g, Carbs- 1g**

Bacon-Wrapped Chicken Sausages

Ingredients

- 1 pound chicken sausages
- 12 slices of bacon

Instructions

Preheat your oven to 375°F (190°C). Wrap each chicken sausage with a slice of bacon and secure with a toothpick if necessary. Arrange the bacon-wrapped chicken sausages on a baking sheet lined with parchment paper. Bake in the oven for 20-25 minutes or until the bacon is crispy and the sausages are cooked. Remove from the oven and let rest for a few minutes before serving. Serve hot.

**Servings-8, Total cooking time -30 mins
Kcal- 250, Proteins- 15g, Fats- 20g, Carbs- 1g**

Ingredients

- 4 boneless, skinless chicken breasts
- 2 tablespoons melted butter
- 1 tablespoon paprika
- 1 teaspoon garlic powder
- 1 teaspoon onion powder
- 1 teaspoon dried thyme
- 1 teaspoon dried oregano
- 1 teaspoon cayenne pepper (optional for extra heat)
- 1 teaspoon black pepper
- 1 teaspoon salt

Instructions

Preheat a cast-iron skillet over medium-high heat. Brush chicken breasts with melted butter and coat with a spice mix of paprika, garlic powder, onion powder, thyme, oregano, cayenne, black pepper, and salt. Cook each side for 5-7 minutes until blackened and the internal temperature reaches 165°F. Let rest before serving.

Servings-4, Total cooking time - 25 mins
Kcal- 250, Proteins- 28g, Fats- 12g, Carbs- 2g

Ingredients

- 1 pound chicken or beef
- 1/2 cup pork rinds, (fine powder)
- 1 large egg
- 1 teaspoon salt
- 1/2 teaspoon black pepper
- Tallow or lard for frying
- Optional: 1 teaspoon garlic powder, 1 teaspoon onion powder

Instructions

Combine the ground meat, crushed pork rinds, egg, salt, pepper, garlic powder, and onion powder in a bowl. Mix until well combined. Form the mixture into small nugget shapes. Heat tallow or lard in a deep skillet or frying pan over medium-high heat. Fry the nuggets in batches, being careful not to overcrowd the pan. Cook for 3-4 minutes on each side until golden brown is cooked through.

Servings-2, Total cooking time -20 mins
Kcal- 350, Proteins- 30g, Fats- 25g, Carbs- 1g

We Value Your Feedback – Share Your Experience!

Thank you for choosing the Carnivore Diet Cookbook for Easy Recipes: 2000 Days of Simple and Delicious Meat-Based Meals with a 30-day Meal Plan. We hope this cookbook has been a valuable resource on your journey to a healthier, meat-based lifestyle. Every recipe, tip, and meal plan was crafted with your success in mind, and we genuinely hope you've enjoyed exploring the delicious possibilities of the carnivore diet.

We value your experience and satisfaction. If this book has helped you simplify your cooking, introduced you to new flavors, or made your carnivore journey more enjoyable, we would be thrilled if you could take a few moments to share your thoughts in a review. Whether it's a favorite recipe, the convenience of the meal plan, or any other aspect you appreciated, your feedback will help us improve our future work and guide others to consider embracing this way of eating.

Leaving a review is quick and easy. Scan the barcode below, and you'll be taken directly to the review page. Your insights and experiences are invaluable to us and to the community of readers who, like you, are seeking to make the most of their carnivore diet journey.

Thank you for being a part of our community and for allowing us to be part of your culinary adventures. Your support and feedback make it all possible. Happy cooking, and may your meals continue to be as nourishing and delicious as ever!

Blake Lucas is a passionate advocate for the carnivore lifestyle, dedicated to sharing the benefits and joys of meat-based nutrition. With years of experience exploring and perfecting carnivore recipes, Blake brings knowledge and creativity to the kitchen.

In "Carnivore Diet Cookbook for Easy Recipes: 2000 Days of Simple and Delicious Meat-Based Meals with a 30-day Meal Plan," Blake combines his expertise with a deep love for simple, wholesome ingredients, providing readers with a comprehensive guide to thriving on a carnivore diet. His recipes are designed to be easy to follow and incredibly satisfying, ensuring anyone can enjoy the health benefits and culinary delights of a meat-centric lifestyle.

When he's not experimenting with new recipes, Blake enjoys sharing his journey and insights with a growing community of carnivore enthusiasts, inspiring others to embrace a delicious and nutritious diet.